Why Are We Here?

The Answer Is Hiding In The Ani Ma'amins

D1715542

Why Are We Here?

The Answer Is Hiding In The Ani Ma'amins

By Rabbi Shlomo Schwartz
Copyright 2022

In grateful memory of my Mother

who first went to work

to pay my yeshiva tuition,

Brundel bas Chaim Yosef & Soreh Faygeh

Known to so many as

Aunty Blanche

Prolog

About The Subtitle

Read the following edited extraction from Wikipedia:

Ani Ma'amin (אני מאמין) "I believe" is a popular capsulation of Rambam's Thirteen Principles (*Yud Gimel Ikkarim)* of the Jewish faith that he introduced to the world.

The anonymous author who wrote the 13 capsules, one for each article of faith, began each with the phrase "*Ani ma'amin be-emunah shelemah*" ("I believe with full faith"), hence their name, the *Ani Ma'amin's.*

Both *Ani Ma'amin* and a poetic version, *Yigdal*, have become optional daily recitations of many Jews. The 12th Ani Ma'amin about Mashiach is often sung in a famous, haunting melody as when Shulem Lemmer sang it at the UN in January 2020.

The popular understanding is that Rambam described the Jewish faith with Thirteen Principles and the Ani Ma'amins are an abbreviated form of them. You may not realize that Rambam himself didn't write the Ani Ma'amins, as expressed in the box above.

You may also not realize that the Ani Ma'amins veer somewhat from Rambam's Thirteen Principles. The reason they veer away may be a reflection of some great criticisms leveled against Rambam and his Principles by other great authorities of his time.

I am a big fan of Rambam (not confident enough to claim "expert" status) and seek to popularize his thoughts to modern readers. My original subtitle was "Don't Believe the Ani Ma'amins"; which I meant in two opposite ways: one positive and one negative.

First, positive. Don't <u>just</u> believe the Ani Ma'amins. Instead, know and internalize them so that they color your every thought. Rambam certainly promoted that kind of intense interest in his Thirteen Principles and the Jewish people bought into that intensity. The handy brevity of the Ani Ma'amins explains how this format became a popular review of Rambam's ideas.

Second, negative. Don't <u>really</u> believe the Ani Ma'amins accurately reflect Rambam's Thirteen Principles describing the Jewish faith. They do not and the errors they propagate may be obscuring the profundity of Rambam's real message.

A Story
This latter interpretation, the negative one, was inspired by a story told to me by my rebbi, R. Yaakov Weinberg, zt"l, a true expert on Rambam. The story was from his childhood when, as a part of the community of Slonim Chasidim, he used to attend his Rebbe's *tish* (Yiddish for table). On special occasions, like Shabbos, his Rebbe would invite all his *Chasidim,* young and old, to his *tish* and share with everybody from his plate, called

sheerayim, which *Chasidim* consider very auspicious to receive. Some consider it akin to dining with angels.

One day, the Rebbe challenged the assembled *Chasidim*, the entire range from young to old, which included some very august members of the community. "Whoever takes on to say every day, without fail, Rambam's Thirteen Principles of Yiddishkeit, will get from me the first *sheerayim* from my plate", said the Rebbe.

The room was silent. Of course, everybody would have loved to be the first to get *sheerayim* from the Rebbe's plate, a big honor, but no one was willing to make the commitment without fail. Everyone understood that the Rebbe meant that the person would say the Ani Ma'amins with concentration and depth of understanding. No one was that sure of themselves that they could pass that grade and they scanned the faces in the crowd to confirm they were not alone. Nobody dared to stand out.

From amidst the silence came my rebbi's 8-year-old voice, "I'll do it". A murmur rose through the crowd. They all knew my rebbi was a child prodigy, but still, they didn't think he was the target of the Rebbe's challenge. They figured the Rebbe wanted some older *chassid* to become an authority on the subject and be a shining example and teacher to the rest—that is why they hesitated. Maybe that was indeed the Rebbe's strategy but he couldn't back down from his promise. He hadn't stipulated any conditions and, anyway, the young boy was the only one to accept the challenge.

Well, weeks passed and every time the Rebbe had a *tish*, before anyone could angle for a piece of *sheerayim* the Rebbe would ask the 8-year-old, "Are you keeping your promise?", he would reply, "of course" and then get the first *sheerayim*. The others were starting to regret they had been so hesitant to accept the offer and some even guessed such regret had been part of the Rebbe's strategy. So it went on and on—until it didn't.

One *tish* when everybody was there, before handing out the *sheerayim* the Rebbe decided to test how well the young boy was doing with his task. "Let's hear how you say the Thirteen Principles," he said. Without hesitation but with a slight grin on his face, my future rebbi started singing *"Yigdal Elokim chai..."* to the conflicted bemusement of all present. They were expecting to hear thirteen Ani Ma'amins but got instead the shorter, sing-song version, called *Yigdal*.

When my rebbi told me this story, he explained that even as a child, he was critical of the Ani Ma'amins; he didn't believe the Rambam wrote the Ani Ma'amins. I had never thought about their authorship, but as soon as he opened the door to the issue, I realized how perceptive he was, even as a child. The writing style of the Ani Ma'amins with its repetitious phrasing—"I believe with perfect faith" over and over again—was completely out of character for Rambam.

Following My Rebbi

Of course, my rebbi knew Rambam's original formulation of the Thirteen Principles inside out and was wholly committed to them. In fact, he gave a series of astounding lecture *shiurs* (all his *shiurs* were astounding) on the *Yud Gimel Ikkarim* (Thirteen Principles) and it might have been around that time that he told me the story.

I have always been fascinated by the *hashkafa* (guiding philosophy) my rebbi taught and have never really stopped pondering and digesting it. I hope that is what is meant when they say "internalize it".

I was also captivated by his method of learning which, to my mind, consisted of a three-pronged attack.

First, let the words of the sages tell you what they said, not what you expected them to say. If you encounter a strange phrase or even just a word, don't allow your preconceived notions to suppress the new idea it may be conveying.

Second, don't settle for vague ideas that only answer part of the question; Torah has to be internally consistent and sound.

Third, if conventional answers don't satisfy the first two requirements, be prepared to think originally. There is something more that has to be brought out—find it.

My rebbi was a very original thinker. That description may be misleading. He didn't invent new ideas — impossible if you are rooted in the Torah. Rather, he invented new ways to present old ideas. In fact, I contend that he composed most of the answers that fueled the Baal Tshuva movement—answers that resolve the religious confusion created by modern western thought.

My rebbi was my hero, my role model; I wanted to be like him. I didn't make a career of being a rebbi but I did volunteer as a teacher rebbi during most of my professional and business career. Consciously or not, I was always devising new Torah insights that addressed contemporary issues. That is why, when I did give a series of classes on Rambam's Thirteen Principles, I found myself developing my own insights, different from those found in existing works, different even from those ascribed to my rebbi.

The astounding *shiurs* on Rambam's Thirteen Principles by my rebbi, R. Yaakov Weinberg, zt"l, were transcribed, edited and published by my classmate of that time, R. Mordechai Blumenfeld, under the title *Fundamentals and Faith* (Feldheim 1991). I used that book to refresh my memory but it didn't answer all my questions.

I have not been the only one with questions. From early on, our Torah giants have vigorously debated each of the thirteen points, as documented by Rabbi J. David Bleich in *With Perfect Faith* (Ktav Publishing House 1983). The Sages whom Rabbi Bleich excerpts are a heavy read because they were addressing the philosophical issues of their day — not ones familiar to me. However, Rabbi Bleich does lead off each point with a perceptive summary of the opinions and I found that very helpful.

Who Is My Audience?

The people I taught were young adults who lacked preconceived respect for the texts or the topic I was teaching. This audience is the huge challenge of our day. I write for them and for those who wish to engage with them. With them in mind, I present ideas that earn respect in their own right by making sense rather than because someone "high up" said it. My overarching premise is that Hashem is palpably real, not just a belief. That is different from most of the world which treats religion as something you have to believe. I insist Torah teaches reality, not belief. I think this conviction led me to uncover how Rambam taught this reality through his Thirteen Principles.

Reality seems so chaotic that just about everyone asks themselves upon occasion, often upon many occasions, "Why Are We Here?". My approach to Rambam's Thirteen Principles answers this question but, to appreciate how it does, you will have to stop believing the Ani Ma'amins and start clarifying them as steps in a logical argument. In other words, don't just believe the Ani Ma'amins, know the basis for them.

Ani Ma'amin and *Yigdal* both attempt to condense Rambam's points. Many people recite one or both each day but may not realize they disagree with each other. I wasn't aware of this disagreement until I started reading to understand instead of reading to get through. I detected a lot of scholarship by the authors of these two works in their decisions of what to capsulize from each point, but I also detected significant departures from Rambam's words which, to my thinking, undermined the logic of the argument he was building. Do you believe the Ani Ma'amins? Don't. Don't accept them as the final word until you consider mine.

Structure Of The Book

I spend a chapter on each of Rambam's Thirteen Principles. Before presenting Rambam's description of his principle, I present the corresponding Ani Ma'amin and Yigdal couplet, as translated by Artscroll, the preeminent English language publisher in the Torah world today. I then critique these texts to justify where my thinking led me.

I then present my translation of Rambam's words, set apart in a box. My translation is fairly literal so as to provide a sense of the original, even though that may make his words sound stilted.

That is not the only reason they may sound stilted. Rambam wrote for the people of his day, addressing their worldview and preconceived notions. Our preconceived notions are different and that is why he may sound somewhat "off" to us. However, my hope is that "the sense of the original" that I have preserved in my translation will help you decide how well I have applied Rambam's wisdom toward bettering our worldview.

The chapter heading will be a question that newcomers to Torah often ask, a question that I think is answered by Rambam's point. The final paragraph(s) of the chapter will start with **Answer to [the chapter's question]**.

Terminology
Re: Artscroll's translation of *ani ma'amin b'emuna shleima* as "I believe with complete faith". The word

ma'amin comes from the root *aleph, mem, nun*, commonly pronounced as *omain*, amen in English. Various forms of this root are used in the sense of faith, trust, confidence, creed, but also builder, professional, nurse, and famously, "so be it". Quite a range of meanings.

I wonder if Hashem didn't provide this word as a derivative of *aleph-mem*, mother. The *nun* at the end is fairly silent, like an afterthought. Assuming Torah language reflects reality — or builds it, which is the same idea from a different direction — most people intuitively trust their mother and consider her the standard against which to measure the world. A mother embodies all the ideas I mentioned: faith, trust, confidence, creed, builder, professional, nurse, and when all else fails, the carry on attitude of "so be it".

Accordingly, if not for Artscroll, I would have translated *ma'amin* as "know intuitively" instead of "believe". That is the kind of awareness one gets from a mother. The "know intuitively" state is acquired by logical inquiry married to acculturation, i.e. living the life. A *Ma'amin* is not someone who has just adapted to his cultural environment because that might include any commonly held fallacy, of which there are many. A *Ma'amin* is someone who has also added logical inquiry to test for propriety. On the other hand, he does not just use logical inquiry because that would treat it as an intellectual conquest, not a personal commitment. A *Ma'amin* lives it and thinks it.

I wanted to make the above point but I never did translate *ma'amin* as "know intuitively" for two reasons. First, out of deference to the people at Artscroll who have proven themselves to be accomplished scholars. They also grappled with translation questions and I hesitate to override them. Second, I wanted my translation to concentrate the reader on how the author of Ani Ma'amin chose to capsulize Rambam's words and not be distracted by his standard opening, which I expect the reader to gloss over as long as I don't draw attention to it.

1 - What Does Science Say About God?

The Familiar Ani Ma'amin: I believe with complete faith in the existence of the Creator, who guides all creatures and who alone made, makes, and will make everything.

My Critique: Right from the start, there are needless additions that suggest Rambam never wrote the Ani Ma'amins. This Ani Ma'amin should have stopped after the first phrase, "the existence of the Creator". The next phrase, "guides all creatures", is an extra concept that is not presented by Rambam until Principle 10. The last phrase, "will make everything", also introduces an extra concept, that of Hashem's eternity, which Rambam delays discussing until Principle 4 (maybe).

I maintain that these "extras" bury the one point that Rambam wanted to start with, from which he would then build his case.

The Yigdal Couplet:
Exalted be the Living God and praised,
He exists – unbounded by time is His existence.

My Critique: This fails to identify Hashem as the Creator. Like Ani Ma'amin, Yigdal concludes on a note about Hashem's eternity, which Rambam saved for later.

Rambam's first description of reality: Be clear about the existence of the Creator. There is a Being complete in all the ways of existence.

He caused all other things to exist. Through Hashem and from Hashem is their survival. Don't even imagine the lack of Hashem's existence; for then all things would dissolve and nothing would survive. But, if the loss of all other things were imagined, the existence of Hashem would not dissolve nor be diminished.

Unity and mastery belong only to Hashem; Hashem is enough. Hashem can be alone without the need for anything else. Everything besides Hashem - such as angels and the bodies of the planets and what is in them and what is below them — all rely on Hashem for their existence.

This is the first principle, as indicated by the first commandment, "I am Hashem, your Lord" (Ex.20:2).

Rambam insists that we first recognize Hashem as the Creator. Not as the Eternal, Holy one, nor as the Lawgiver, nor as the Redeemer, although he would agree with each one. Not even as the Father which would imply the Creator, but also include a personal relationship. He will get to that, too, but for starters, just recognize Hashem as the Creator.

Rambam starts this way for two reasons. First, he wanted to refute all the philosophers and scientists of his day who claimed the universe was always there, it was eternal — there was no "Creator". Second, he wanted to describe reality and reality would be quite different if the Universe (Earth and everything else) had always been there when Hashem came along and decided to "work" with it. In that case, the Universe would be just as real as Hashem is. It is not, as I shall expound in the coming pages.

The philosophers and scientists of Rambam's day were sophisticated thinkers so I am surprised they insisted that the Universe had always been there. They were certainly aware that change was always happening and, for every change, they could discover a cause. How then could the sum total of all the changes—the Universe—have no cause? Hashem is the easy answer because Hashem is outside the system and, therefore, could be unchanging and without cause. Nevertheless, many refused to concede to this for the longest time because it is hard to change conventional thinking. They conceded just recently.

Recently, science has finally accepted that the Universe was not always there—that it had a start—because they discovered the Big Bang. Now, the scientists will tell you that before the Big Bang there was nothing—no energy, no matter, not even space. So who or what started the Big Bang? Scientists still won't concede to talk about Hashem so they use a different name, Quantum Mechanics.

Quantum mechanics are the laws that govern subatomic particles and forces, at which level science has proven something can come from nothing. These are the laws that produced the Big Bang. Now that these laws have been scientifically proven, we no longer need to <u>believe</u> in Creation, we can <u>know</u> it as well as we know anything else. We just have to realize that Creation-from-nothing occurs at the subatomic level.

In this way, scientists are actually discovering some fascinating details about how Hashem created everything. That last statement might shock you because conventional wisdom teaches that science explains everything without needing Hashem. All such educators and promoters of conventional wisdom should be admonished for refusing to see how new scientific discoveries lend exciting new dimensions to ancient wisdom.

Sometimes, all it takes is a new frame of mind. The insights that follow were inspired by a Youtube video narrated by Gerald Schroeder titled *Believe in God in 5 Minutes (Scientific Proof)* (you can also search its alternative title, *God Discovered in 5 Minutes*). Gerald Schroeder is an established scientist, the author of *Genesis and the Big Bang* (Bantam Doubleday, 1991), and a long-time lecturer at Aish HaTorah in Jerusalem.

Quantum Mechanics Created The Universe
Scientists say the laws of quantum mechanics kick-started the universe. Scientists don't like to spell this out but this means the laws of quantum mechanics pre-date the universe. Pre-dating the universe means they pre-date anything physical so they themselves cannot be physical. Thus, the two words "quantum mechanics" describe the non-physical forces or powers that started our physical universe. But this scientific name, quantum mechanics, strips these forces of personality. We should not be surprised because that is so "scientific".

Scientists avoid discussing "personality" because it is not yet scientifically measurable. Certainly not in an absolute sense. They also avoid discussing "intelligence" even though intelligence has been measured for some time, because the measure is only in relative terms - this person compared to that person — and even then, it is imprecise. Accordingly, scientists will not assign the terms "personality" or "intelligence" to the quantum forces behind creation. It falls to us religious thinkers to realize how that obscures the reality they have discovered.

Despite the absence of precise measures, personality and intelligence are real. Together they are goal-oriented. Personality defines the goal and intelligence finds a way to reach the goal. The goal we are talking about is the complex universe we inhabit. Scientists used to argue that the same "goal", our complex universe, could be reached by accident through random events over billions of years. They don't make this argument so easily anymore, but not because of any doubt about the billions of years.

The scientific evidence for a 14 billion-year-old universe is brilliantly reconciled to the Torah account of six days of creation by Schroeder in *Genesis and The Big Bang*. To do this, he applies Einstein's teaching that time travels at different speeds for observers in different gravity zones. (As astounding as this seems, Einstein's teaching has since been proven.) Schroeder's book mathematically matches the billions of years science estimates it took to form each stage of Earth's evolution to the exact same stage described by the Torah account of six days.

Our gravity zone on Earth gives us the sense of billions of years of time elapsed since the Big Bang. The gravity zone at the edge of the universe would give a person standing there the perspective of six days for the same period. Since humans don't appear on the scene until the end of the story of Creation, that story is told from Hashem's perspective which is figuratively at the edge, looking in; thereafter, the perspective changes to our own.

Thus, religious thinkers can accept the scientific age of the universe. Now, we need to get scientific thinkers to overcome the idea that our world developed through random events.

Recent discoveries in the fields of cosmology, inorganic chemistry, and microbiology, to name a few, have revealed that life requires the perfect alignment of far more factors than previously imagined. Very much more. Prodigiously much more. So much more that even if there were a billion times a billion of years — which there were not, only 14 billion or so according to science, the statistical probability of all the necessary factors aligning perfectly to create Life by accident is zero, non-existent. That is a scientific fact.

Here are a few examples I extracted from Youtube videos of the Dallas Science Faith Conference 2020.

Cosmologist Stephen Meyer (PhD. Cambridge University) has shown that several factors controlled how the Big Bang unfolded. They were: the speed of light, the expansion rate of the universe, the two nuclear forces, one strong and one weak, the forces of gravity and electromagnetism, the ratio of protons to electrons, and solar luminosity. The precise values of each of these factors could all have been different than they are — the values could have varied as infinitely as the dials on your stove. Yet if any of these values were even slightly different than they are, life would have been impossible. The scientific probability of all the values aligning by accident to support life is zero.

Inorganic chemist James Tour (PhD. Purdue University) has shown that <u>no one</u> can explain how even a single living cell could evolve from its lifeless components — there are too many steps involved. Any step that resulted in failure would have necessitated starting from the beginning without the benefit of knowing that the failure must be avoided next time because inorganic components cannot "know" anything. Thus, evolutionary progress from non—life to life is impossible.

Microbiologist Michael Behe (PhD. University of Pennsylvania) has shown that there are molecular machines such as the flagellum that are essential for life but display irreducible complexity. That means they cannot have evolved by successive small modifications to pre-existing functional systems because a less-complex system would serve no function. The evolution would have been aborted by its own rules of adaptation necessities. Thus, they had to appear already intact, an impossible accident.

(The argument of irreducible complexity is an old one, previously based on an eye or a bird's wing. For example, what benefit could early versions of a wing provide so that it would keep developing into something that finally allowed flight? Nevertheless, the die-hard atheists theorized possible scenarios. But now, looking at the molecular level, such theories are much, much less believable.)

These findings have become so convincing that atheists have resorted to a desperate maneuver to explain how the universe could still be a random event, despite the impossible odds against it. They propose that instead of Hashem purposefully creating the universe there is some mindless source constantly but haphazardly creating an infinite number of Big Bangs.

Among an infinite number, every possible combination will happen. Therefore, among all these Big Bangs, one would definitely incorporate the right combination of factors to produce our world, and we must be that one.

The beauty of this argument is that it cannot be disproven. By definition, we can never investigate another universe, let alone the source of all universes, because an ability to investigate it would make it part of our universe. But that definition is its downfall, as well. To be considered scientific—and we do want to stay within the bounds of science, do we not?—a hypothesis must allow itself to be disproven and this one does not. Scientists know this and that is why I earlier called it a desperate maneuver.

Since life did happen and it couldn't have been an accident, scientists who are prepared to face reality must admit that quantum mechanics made the complexities of life (intelligence) happen as a result of a goal (personality) because it couldn't have happened by chance. The Torah in *Breishis* calls that intelligent personality *ALoHYM*, a term that doesn't really stray far from the idea of quantum mechanics, a set of laws that started the universe, as I will soon demonstrate.

First, let me acknowledge that my English spellings of Hebrew words do not conform to normal conventions. The reason is my purpose is different. Normally, English renditions seek to convey the sound of the Hebrew word. I wish, though, to convey the original Hebrew letters and, to do this, I use uppercase characters. Many times this results in unpronounceable words because the vowel sounds were understood and not represented by letters. In those cases, I insert a lowercase character to convey the sound of the word. I represent the Hebrew letter *shin* with an underlined <u>SH</u> to indicate it is one character. All this is to show how the words are built up.

Revelations From the Holy Names of Hashem

Consider the first three Hebrew words in the Torah: "*BRAy<u>SH</u>YS BaRA ALoHYM...*", usually translated as: "In the beginning, Hashem created…".

The first word, *BRAy<u>SH</u>YS*, means "in the beginning".

The middle word, *BaRA*, means "created". It comes before the subject, Hashem, for a very telling reason; Torah focuses on action, ie. behavior, and so usually puts the verb, the behavior, before the subject.

(This variation from English syntax was pointed out to me by my non-Jewish professor of Hebrew 101. He observed that the culture behind the English language values material things more than behavior and so puts the material subject first. The Torah puts the verb first to show that behavior is more important.)

The last word, *ALoHYM*, is one of Hashem's seven holy names — holy in the sense that they are spoken and written according to special rules of reverence. It is usually translated as God or Lord. I will soon discuss which is the better translation, God or Lord.

I will also need to discuss three more of the holy names. They are: *AiL,* and *ALO'aH* (see below) and *YHVH* (Eternity/Infinity/God — this is the holiest name and we don't even pronounce it so I haven't given it lowercase vowels; non-Jews made out of it "Jehovah" and now often pronounce it "Yaweh", but neither is the correct pronunciation — Hashem is a substitute).

Of the seven holy names, Hashem in the first story of creation is only called *ALoHYM* (Gen. 1:1-2:3). The second story, the one about the Garden of Eden, introduces Hashem as *YHVH* for the first time and after that, the two names are usually used together. It is so unusual to find Hashem called only *ALoHYM* that we have to ask, "What secret message is the first story hinting to us?"

Three Names Of Hashem Come From One
I suggest the answer lies in treating *ALoHYM* as a composite of two of the other seven holy names, *AiL* and *ALO'aH*.

AiL is often paired with *ELYON* to mean "the supreme power"; alone *AiL* means force or power, so it is the most natural name of Hashem. *AiL* is the shortest holy name of Hashem, consisting of only two letters. I find it fascinating that the same two Hebrew letters, *AL*, also form two other words when pronounced more softly as either "el" or "ul". *AL* sounded as "el" means "to" for describing the movement of one object "to" another whereas *AL* sounded as "ul" means "don't".

"To" and "don't" seem to be very different words until they are grouped with the more emphatic pronunciation of *AiL*, meaning a force of power. Then all three shed light on each other. As Sir Isaac Newton observed, a "force — *AiL*" can only be observed by the relationship of one object "to" another.

Think about that for a moment. The very essence of a "force" lies in its relation "to" something else.

The next step is to realize that some relationships are harmful; in that case, the advice would be "don't".

Torah Hebrew considers its alphabet the building blocks of creation, of reality. That is why we should not be surprised to find that the same two letters of *AL* describe one reality that we perceive in three different ways, namely, "force", "to" (good relationship) and "don't" (bad relationship).

All Hebrew nouns are assigned gender, either male or female. This is more than just a grammatical rule. It is Hashem's way of assuring us that everything created has a role to play which is another way of saying it has a personality. Male and female are the two main personality types so every noun has a gender to hint at its role type. Many nouns have both a male and female form to reflect the same basic entity in a male or female role. For example, boy and girl are both humans but have different personalities which are reflected by their Hebrew nouns of *YeLeD* (boy) and *YaLDaH* (girl), both having the same letters YLD except for the extra H at the end which is the hallmark of a feminine noun.

AiL, defined above, is a male noun. *ALO'aH* is another holy name of Hashem. It starts with the softer *AL* and ends with "*H*", the common ending for feminine nouns. The "*O*" is a vowel letter for pronouncing the "*H*" leaving only the first two letters, *AL*, to signify meaning. As stated above, one pronunciation of *AL* means force, but in this case with the female ending of *H*, it means a female force. Femininity, if you like.

That certainly conforms to reality. Male and female outlooks are often different, sometimes as forces of contention and other times as powers of assistance. Hashem, who started it all, must be capable of both male and female outlooks. Hence, a separate name to identify the male powers of Hashem, *AiL*, and the female powers of Hashem, *ALO'aH*.

By now you should notice that the name *ALoHYM*, starts with *AL*, continues very similarly to *ALO'aH*, and ends with *YM*. *YM* is the standard suffix attached to a male word to indicate plural. (A different suffix is used to indicate plural for female nouns.) Since there is no neuter in Hebrew, the plural for a mixed group of males and females together had to be one of the already existing forms. The rule was chosen to reflect reality; since males dominate more often than females, use the male suffix YM.

Taking all of the above, I understand *ALoHYM* to mean the sum and source of all powers (*AL*) embedded into the world, powers we describe as male or female. For example, natural forces can be overpowering like lightning strikes and tornadoes (male) or nurturing like raindrops and sunshine (female).

The above explains why *ALoHYM,* the plural describing a group of males and females — in this case, male and female powers — is the only holy name used in the first story of creation. It is because that was when all the male and female components were initially put together. For this reason, I think the better translation of *ALoHYM* is Lord rather than God or Hashem because a lord is a person of power whereas God conveys a much broader concept that includes relating, forgiving, saving, and the like. Relating, forgiving, and saving require a patient long-term view which is why I contend the word God should be used to translate YHVH (Eternity/Infinity).

It is worthwhile to note that far east philosophy has something similar to *ALoHYM* in Yin and Yang which also represents males and females, among other opposites. Comparing these terms to *ALoHYM* teaches us something.

Yin and Yang describe forces that both oppose and complement each other, such as bright and dark, sun and moon, passive and active. These are indeed realities so it is not surprising that wise men all over the world discovered these opposites and used them to make sense of their world.

However, reality tends to be misunderstood without the benefit of revelation, such as recorded in the Torah. Yin and Yang describe the universe as governed by cosmic dualities, sometimes competing and sometimes complementing. That is confusing. Worse, each duality is apparently independent of the others leading to a sense of chaos. Chaos can infect the thinking of even the world's greatest minds, causing them to concoct outrageous proposals to solve their problems. In contrast, *ALoHYM* acknowledges the dualities but explains they are all in harmony and work together under the control of one entity, Hashem. Torah revelation assures us there is abiding harmony in our world. Once we are so assured, harmony is much easier to detect.

The conclusion to date: Quantum mechanics describes the forces that created our universe from nothing. Unfortunately, the description is somewhat sterile — a bunch of laws. Too many statistical improbabilities were overcome to deny purposeful intelligence. The terminology in *Breishis*, especially *ALoHYM*, identifies underlying intelligence, even of types we call male and female. Now, to match the intelligence, I have to find the underlying purpose.

What I Learned From An Animal Documentary

ALoHYM not only intelligently pursued the goal of making life, but it also did so with gusto. Even a rudimentary knowledge of nature makes you aware of the myriad variety of life on this planet. However, awareness does not always impress and I am an example of that. I knew about the variety of life but it didn't impact me until I watched *March of the Penguins* which won the 2006 Oscar for best documentary feature. This was a well-deserved reward to Laurent Chalet and Jerome Maison who spent a full year filming in frozen Antarctica.

Watch the film and you will witness, as if you were there, the annual mating journey of Antarctica's emperor penguins. They waddle and slide over 60 miles of ice to get to their ancestral mating ground. Sixty miles! The scenes I remember best are those showing over a thousand penguins huddling together for warmth during a -60 C (-80 F) storm. They cannot seek shelter for fear of damaging the single egg that they are warming between their feet. The penguins huddle like this for two months! These are the males! The females, meanwhile, return to the sea where they hunt and gorge themselves, storing up enough body fat reserves to return at the end of hatching to feed their young and relieve the males.

Watching these scenes left me astonished at the variety of life on this planet; the brutal cold endured, the huddling for two months, and the reversal of roles between males and females, among others. All the while, I was subconsciously comparing them to more familiar life forms, such as farm animals, pet animals, even jungle animals — endlessly different life forms, different environments, different homing instincts, different eating habits, and so on. I marveled at how much Hashem loves creating different variations on a theme.

And then it hit me. That is exactly how the Torah starts, "BRAySHYS BaRA ALoHYM — In the beginning, Hashem created..." (Gen. 1:1). I never thought of it that way before, but it is actually describing Hashem's personality. Hashem loves to create!

This is exactly how Rambam starts his description of reality, by describing Hashem as a creator. Hashem created everything, all the elements and forces, all the atoms and molecules, all the galaxies and stars, all the plants and microorganisms, all the species of animals, fish and birds, all the instinctual behaviors, everything.

The Creative Urge

What's in it for Hashem to have created the universe? Maybe just to express a creative urge. I think the Torah text hints at this with a stylistic trick. I have previously explained the Torah phrase *BRAySHYS BaRA ALoHYM*. The middle word, *BaRA*, is three Hebrew letters that mean "created". The first word, *BRAySHYS*, means "in the beginning", but notice it starts with the same three letters as *BaRA* — remember, the lowercase letters don't appear in the text. Stylistically, the Torah text hints at Hashem's love of creating by embedding the idea of creating in the first three letters. Created, created — the emphasis is on creating. The first revelation about Hashem's personality is that Hashem loves creating. (Another personality revelation is that Hashem likes to hide behind clues for us to discover.)

I find in the text another hint about the act of creating. Imagine Hashem before creating. There is nothing but Hashem. Nothing else. No universe, no space, no time, not even numbers. No need for numbers because there is nothing to count. There is no need for Hashem to be number 1 because there is no number 2. Thus, the first thing to create would be the number 2, which is a concept. It is the concept of something other than Hashem.

In Hebrew, letters are used to represent numbers. The number 1 is signified by the first letter, *Aleph*, the number 2 by the second letter, *Bais*, and so on. Now notice that the Torah describes the beginning of creation with text that begins with the letter *B*, the number 2. This supports what I said above! The first thing Hashem had to create was the number 2, the concept of something, anything, other than Hashem, even just a number. This is another example of hiding clues. The first two words of Genesis start with B, the number 2; only then comes the word *ALoHYM* starting with A, the number 1.

How did *ALoHYM* first create? Scientists tell us it was with the Big Bang (ironically, the B's appear even in English, two of them). Out of nowhere/nothing, Quantum Mechanics created the Big Bang of very intense energy that quickly blew up (expanded) into heat, light, and space for the formation of simple atoms such as hydrogen and helium. These inanimate things kept expanding and transforming into other things of greater complexity and interplay to form the galaxies, stars, and the world we live in. Every step of the way introduced a design of ever greater sophistication, testifying to a master delighted with building the craft at hand. But this is only part of the story, the physical part.

The Onset Of Spirituality
The Torah text tells us the rest of the story, the non-physical part, but this message has usually been obscured by translation. To show this I will use the most widely known translation of the first few verses (except I changed the word "God" to "the Lord", as explained above).

"In the beginning, the Lord created the heaven and the earth. And the earth was without form, and void, and darkness was upon the face of the deep. And the spirit of the Lord moved upon the face of the waters. And the Lord said: Let there be light and there was light" (Gen. 1:1-3).

This was the first day and the translation implies the earth was created before the light. But, for day three, we read: "And the Lord said, Let the water under the heaven be gathered together unto one place, and let the dry land appear: and it was so. And the Lord called the dry land earth…" (Gen. 1:9-10).

Why is Hashem assigning the name "earth" to the dry land when earth already existed on day one? The answer is that "earth" on day one does not mean the earth that falls between your fingers when you pick up a clump of dry land; it doesn't even mean planet earth.

Torah Hebrew has a limited vocabulary so it uses the same word to describe different stages of a concept. I showed this above with the three meanings of "force", "to" and "don't" for the one Hebrew word of *AL*. The Torah word E<u>R</u>e<u>TZ</u>, earth, is another example of the same phenomenon.

The "earth" of day three is the later stage of dry land but the "earth" of day one is referring to the first stage of all physical matter, especially the inanimate aspect of it. On day one, the Torah tells us, all physics was created: energy, mass, and space. It tells us this through stories because that is stage one of human learning. Today, scientists prefer a more mathematical depiction and so they careen through the debris of the Big Bang explosion while repeating the mantra of $E=mc^2$.

If "earth" of day one means all physical matter, what does "heaven" of day one mean? In the phrase "heaven and earth", "heaven" must mean "non-earth". If "earth" of day one is all physical matter then "heaven" - non-earth - is all non-physical matter — what we call spiritual matter.

This answers why Hashem re-named the physical firmament (sky) on day two (Gen.1:5) and called it "heaven", something non-physical. We tend to think physical things are all there is because that is all our five senses can detect. With the sky, Hashem suggested something beyond us, by providing an endless horizon that looks non-physical (even though we have learned it really is physical). By naming the sky "heaven", we are constantly reminded of the original heaven, the original non-physical. We call it the spiritual world.

The Torah text even helps us define the content of that spiritual world. By mentioning heaven first in the opening verse, the text implies that the spiritual, non-physical world was needed before the creation of the physical world. (It wasn't to assign importance because a later verse, Gen. 2:4, mentions the two as first "heaven and earth" and then as "earth and heaven" implying their equal importance.)

In our reality, before crafting something useful we first have to conceive an image of our goal along with a plan to achieve it. Neither the image nor the plan is physical. They may be depicted physically on paper but their essence exists mentally, without the depiction. The image and plan are spiritual entities. The same applies to rules that govern an object. Some rules are made by Hashem such as the strength and weight of the object; some are man-made rules such as who may use it and under what circumstances. But, all types of rules are spiritual entities because they exist in the abstract.

If you find the above description of the spiritual world too out-of-the-box, consider the following. Which part of a person conceives a goal, a plan to achieve it, and rules for deploying it? Isn't it the personality and intelligence of the person? Some call that combination "the mind" and some call it "the soul". Mind or soul, there lies the seat of all things we normally think of as spiritual such as love, ideals, art and music appreciation, and so on. All of these are non-physical in their essence.

The Onset Of Good And Bad
Having said that, note that other items also qualify for that list of spirituals even though they seem quite different. I am thinking of items such as hate, chaos, and aloofness. These are also not physical, so they too are spiritual entities. The fact that some spiritual qualities are <u>not good</u> may come as a surprise but it was already taught in the Torah, as follows.

Day 2 in *Breishis*, the day we are introduced to the sky which teaches us about our spiritual dimension, is the only day of the first six that is <u>not labeled good</u>. On every other day of creation, a verse mentions "Hashem saw that it was good". The absence of this phrase from day 2 implies that spirituality includes some things that are not good. Jewish tradition explains that day 2 was not labeled good because it introduced division into the world in the form of a separation between the waters above and the waters below.

This phrasing choice teaches us that division or separation is the granddaddy of all bad spiritual things — it models the arrogance of "I can do this alone" meaning "I can separate myself from others". This is the antithesis of reality because nothing works alone; all items are the product of the one creator and were only differentiated by name so we could appreciate the harmony in which they work.

The takeaway from this is a thought-provoking response to a person who says they are very spiritual, just not religious. We can gently point out that they are not necessarily painting themselves in a good light. The job of religion is to distinguish between good and bad spiritual forces. By rejecting religion they are convincing themselves that they have a better answer than all the generations and scholars who preceded them — a conviction that betrays a certain amount of arrogance. Arrogance easily evolves into hate, chaos, and aloofness, the examples of spiritual evils mentioned earlier. This is not the self-image they thought they were advertising when they described themselves as spiritual, just not religious. We ought to encourage them to reconsider religion and look for the one that makes the most sense. A reality religion, meaning a religion based on realities that one can recognize from personal experience and logic, would identify positive spiritual qualities for them to pursue. That would be the Torah.

Is There a "There" There?

I find in the Torah text another hint to the recent scientific discoveries about the composition of our universe. The Torah word for heaven and sky is _SHoMaYiM_. The same word denotes the singular, heaven or sky, and the plural, heavens or skies. Singular and plural expressions with the same word are not so unusual.

What is unusual is that _SHoMaYiM_ is not referring to a pair of things as do almost all other words that end in "_aYiM_". For example, _AyNaYiM_ means a pair of eyes, _YaDaYiM_ means a pair of hands, _RaGLaYiM_ means a pair of legs. Not just two, but a pair that work together. Why did _SHoMaYiM_ break this mold?

Now, quantum mechanics provides a template for understanding _SHoMaYiM_ as a pair of things. The first part of _SHoMaYiM_ is _SHoM_ which means "there". I am inspired here by an amusing phrase that has become popular, "there is no 'there' there". It means, there is nothing of substance there. I quote it not for its logic, but for its humorous introduction of a pair of "there"s.

Scientists have determined that one key characteristic of energy from the Big Bang is that it behaves like a wave. Basically, a wave is a crest and a trough — two positions, two locations, two "there"s. "There"s are not physical and I have already equated things non-physical to spiritual. Thus, it might be that the reality of the energy waves created by the Big Bang, the pair of "there"s, is described in the Torah text by *SHoMaYiM*, the heaven, the spiritual world. How adroit of the Torah text to reflect this reality of a pair, a crest and a trough, in the name of a thing.

(The above is not a proof of anything, just a cute breadcrumb trail left by the author, Hashem. Another such cute hint may lie in the word for water, *MaYiM*, the very thing where we first experience waves; it too ends with "*aYiM*", a pair of "there"s.)

Answer to: What Does Science Say About God?
People who think rationally, scientists for example, have always known there must be something permanent that started everything. Scientists used to think that the universe, itself, was that permanent something. With the Big Bang discovery, they reassigned the starting role to quantum mechanics. That is their drab name for Hashem.

Breishis teaches us something about *ALoHYM*, a name that more colorfully alludes to Hashem's intelligence and personality. *Breishis* also teaches us that Hashem loves to create and the universe is a byproduct of that love-to-create. "Bi-product" is a better spelling because the universe displays a binary character; it exists on 2 planes, spiritual and physical, is composed of the 2 parts of a wave, highs and lows, and reflects 2 views of the world, male and female. All of this—because the universe starts as 2nd to Hashem.

Our reality is 2ndary to Hashem. We cannot exist without Hashem. Probably not wise to try.

2 - What Was Hashem Thinking?

<u>The Familiar Ani Ma'amin</u>: I believe with complete faith that the Creator, blessed is His Name, is unique and there is no uniqueness like His in any way, and that He alone is our God, Who was, Who is, and Who always will be.

My Critique: If the primary goal of the Ani Ma'amins was to summarize Rambam's points, this one should have been shorter. It should have just repeated Rambam's main point about unity, namely that Hashem is "the same cause of everything". Adding "Who was, Who is, and Who always will be" doesn't explain the uniqueness; it only repeats the eternity concept already mentioned in the previous Ani Ma'amin.

True, Rambam also inserted into his first statement an extra mention of unity even though this seems to be the place to say it. In his defense, I suggest that the unity of the first statement refers to Hashem as the only Creator whereas here he emphasizes the singularity of Hashem. In other words, Hashem was the only Creator because there was no other entity that could create or be used to create.

<u>The Yigdal Couplet</u>:
He is One – and there is no unity like His Oneness –
Inscrutable and infinite is His Oneness;

My Critique: This statement does not connect Hashem's singularity to Creation.

Rambam's second description of reality: Be clear about the unity of Hashem who is the same cause of everything.

Hashem is not like one of a sequence and not like one of a type. Hashem is not like one body consisting of many [smaller] parts and not even like a simple body which is numerically one [but] can be infinitely divided. Rather Hashem is one in a unity that has no parallel.

This is the second principle, as indicated by the verse, "Listen Israel, Hashem is our Lord, Hashem is one." (Deut. 6:4)

In the next few statements (chapters for us), **Rambam** goes on to further describe Hashem. Obviously, no one could ever fully describe Hashem so these must be the details about Hashem that he feels are essential for us to understand our reality. Rambam also carefully chose the order of his presentation. His first description of reality — that Hashem loves to create and is a prolific creator — raises a question: what did Hashem use to create all these things?

Scientists tell us that everything is composed of energy. All the material things we see in the universe are different forms of energy. This is the meaning of the famous equation $E=mc^2$ in which **E** stands for energy, **m** stands for mass or material things and **c** stands for the speed of light. Expressed in a different order, $m=E/c^2$, any mass or material thing is composed of energy slowed way down by twice dividing it with the speed of light.

Did the energy co-exist with Hashem, the creator, and then Hashem used the energy to make the world? No, because that would mean the energy was always there but the Big Bang discovery tells us that the energy appeared all of a sudden. It wasn't there before.

Science can pinpoint when it first appeared but also insists it wasn't there before that. Apparently, Hashem (quantum mechanics) created the energy and then used that to form everything else, but how did Hashem create the energy? The scientific answer is: out of nothing.

Nothing Is Everywhere
Note that "nothing" is the scientific answer. "Nothing" is more real than it sounds because "nothing" is more common than we realize. I remember from high school physics that all material is made up of atoms that have three major components, neutrons, protons, and

electrons. (These days they talk about up-quarks and down-quarks, but the idea remains the same.) In the center nucleus are no-charge neutrons and positively charged protons. Around the perimeter is a cloud of electrons, negatively charged. The positive and negative charges balance each other. These three components insist on staying together. When we try to split them, we get an atom bomb.

Atoms are too small to see with the naked eye but pretend you could enlarge an atom by pinching your fingers and then spreading them apart, the same way you enlarge a picture on your touchscreen. Every component would grow by the same degree of expansion.

Suppose you enlarge the center nucleus to the size of an orange. If you did, you may be surprised to learn that the electron cloud surrounding it would now be four miles away! Even more surprising is that between the nucleus and the electron there would be nothing. There would have to be nothing entering that space because, if something did enter it, that would split the atom and produce an atom bomb, as stated above.

Four miles of "nothing" surrounding the orange-sized nucleus! Obviously, the biggest part of the atom-something is nothing. This teaches us something about reality: every physical object is made up of atoms that are almost completely nothing. The atoms are so small and so determined to stay together that we cannot detect all that nothing-space but our reality is mostly nothing.

It might even be completely nothing. What is the energy that makes up the atom? It is a positive charge surrounded by a negative charge. Plus one minus one equals zero. Stated in reverse, $0=1-1$. You might say that Hashem took a piece of nothing (zero), split it into two, called one half a positive proton ($+1$) and the other half a negative electron (-1), and just by naming them so, got something.

The act of creation was an act of the mind. Hashem made up the idea of two halves of zero and created something. But "really", it is nothing. (The previous chapter discussed Creation starting with two things, Heaven and Earth. This is another example of Hashem creating the universe out of 2, two halves.)

Hashem Is One Means Hashem Is The Only Reality
Hashem is the only one. There is nothing else. We must conclude this because it was only in Hashem's mind that everything was created. In Hashem's mind, zero was conceptualized into two parts and something came into being. In other words, Hashem is the only reality and everything else is a figment of Hashem's imagination. This explains how Rambam could earlier say that if

Hashem would cease, everything would cease. There is no existence without Hashem actively imagining it.

You might consider this belittling — that we are just a figment of Hashem's imagination — but really the concept is fantastically energizing! It means that Hashem is actively aware of everything we do, all the time. It has to be that way because if we weren't in Hashem's awareness, we would disappear. This is not really a new thought to religious people who have always preached about a Hashem who knows everything. But they never could explain it in existential terms.

Now, science explains the connection between our existence and Hashem's knowledge. Springboarding from the immense data found within DNA, the latest scientific theories basically equate mass/material with information, positive and negative "ideas". Scratch below the surface and there is nothing of real substance except data. Our skeleton, our nervous system, our blood vessels, organs, and neural network, our whole being is a collection of related data inside a database that comprises the universe. Stated from the opposite direction, **Hashem's mind maintains all the thoughts** that appear as separate physical entities. (An easy way to learn more about the universe as a database is to watch Youtube videos by scientists Stephen Meyer,

Michael Behe, and James Tour, particularly the videos from the Dallas Science Faith Conference 2020.)

Hashem Has To Be As Aware As Google

Through the centuries, the same idea of Hashem's awareness has been expressed by saying there is a personal Hashem, a Hashem that knows each person.

Skeptics have ignored this claim by asserting "Hashem has more things to worry about than me". This assertion rings hollow today in the face of our experience with search engines such as Google. Any question to Google gets at least 26 million answers in less than a second. That is true for each of the approximately 63 million users accessing Google every second. Google is something we invented. If Google is never too "tired" or busy to respond instantaneously to any question from any user, then surely that would be even more true for Hashem who

"invented" us who

invented Google.

Another important corollary of this reality of Hashem imagining us is that everything, and especially every person, has a purpose. Since we are all imagined by Hashem, there must be a reason for including us in the imagination. We each have a purpose. We each fit in. Otherwise, the imaginer, Hashem, would cease to include us.

Finding Our Purpose

If we are each included, why is our purpose so difficult to pinpoint? Science explains it—existence started through quantum mechanics at the subatomic level, far below our normal perception. The start of everything, including our purpose, was below our normal perception.

On the other hand, our intelligence and curiosity propel us to investigate. Occasionally, our investigation yields a justification for ourselves. If we can do it sometimes, we can do it more times. The knowledge that we are imagined, from the subatomic level up, propels us to justify ourselves to an ever greater level of detail. The devil is not in the details, we are!

We should never fret about not fitting into the overall scheme of things because a key corollary of "Hashem being one" is that everything must be in harmony. Whatever purpose Hashem had in imagining us was not confined to just us because Hashem is imagining everything else, the entire environment, at the same time. It must all fit in.

Are You Thinking What I'm Thinking?

Maybe you will ask, if Hashem is imagining it all, then are my thoughts my own? To answer, I have to ask you a question. Have you ever made up a story? Could be any kind of story, from a bedtime story to an outright lie to get out of something. Upon reviewing that incident, you may remember how your story suddenly took a turn or twist that you thought of just as you were telling it. It was as if the story had a mind of its own. But it didn't. It was your story coming from your mind. Yet the story did have a mind of its own because the twist or turn came out of nowhere — your mind hadn't planned it.

I explain this as follows: When your story came up with that sudden twist or turn, your mind decided to allow it and then made it fit in. That begins to explain how Hashem works with you. The difference is that when you make up a story, you may only be able to handle one sudden turn or twist at a time; Hashem can handle a lot more and they are called your thoughts. You are Hashem's story and you come up with a new thought and then Hashem decides whether to allow it. If yes, then it is fitted in.

We tell ourselves that it all fits in because collective wisdom has proclaimed it. But we often don't feel it. We often feel that we don't fit in, there are too many things opposing us. At such times, it is very useful to remember that opposite forces are the very nature of existence. Protons and electrons are not "alike", but they work together to create our reality. Of course, they have no choice but to work together while we do have other options. Whatever we choose, our composure is greatly enhanced by knowing that these options were presented intentionally by Hashem.

Granted, it may seem that Hashem is not aware of every move we make because we don't perceive Hashem reacting. That is because it is hard to notice something that is always there. Hashem continually imagines us and reacts to us in a consistent and predictable manner. We call that Nature and reserve the name Hashem for events out of the ordinary. But Nature is not separate from Hashem which, by the way, is why it is not always predictable.

Don't deny Nature's fickleness by citing our lack of awareness of all the factors at play. Don't say, "if only we had known this and that, we could have predicted the outcome", because knowledge of all the factors will not do it. Quantum mechanics tells us that even with all the factors known, the result is not predictable at the subatomic level. These features of Nature are what the Torah calls *ALoHYM*, one of the seven holy names of Hashem, as explained in Chapter 1.

Breishis also tells us we were made in the image of *ALoHYM*. That is the name used. Oh! That identifies the source of the sudden twist and turn in a story we make up. It comes from the subatomic quantum mechanics of our subconscious. The world will always seem unpredictable to us but Hashem will always make it fit.

Answer to: What Was Hashem Thinking? This question was modeled after the colloquial phrase "what was he thinking" to capture the reader's interest. It is usually asked by a person who thinks they know better than the other guy, in this case, better than Hashem. The questioner thinks they could have come up with a better design, better goals, better morals, or whatever. A person would have to consider themselves on a somewhat equal footing with Hashem to conceive the question. The easiest path to such delusion is to picture Hashem as a human. That is why there are so many mitzvahs against carved images. My description of Hashem as a body-less mind with an active imagination should block such delusions from arising.

The correct form of the question is, "what <u>is</u> Hashem thinking?" and the answer is, us. All of us and all the universe are the current thought of Hashem. Necessarily, there can only be one thinker, ie. singular in every which way, alone, unified and unique.

We exist only in Hashem's imagination. But don't take that as a putdown. Being nothing more than a figment of Hashem's imagination has its advantages.

First, Hashem's imagination is all there is and all there ever will be so we are as good as it gets. We are as real as it gets.

Second, Hashem's imagination never ceases so we have Hashem's unceasing attention. Really.

Third, Hashem's focused attention means there is a reason for each of us to be here. Considering the number of variables Hashem is juggling, our purpose must be quite intricate.

Considering our lifelong drive to find purpose, Hashem must be imagining we can find our purpose. That is a really comforting thought!

3 - Why Can't We See Hashem?

<u>The Familiar Ani Ma'amin</u>: I believe with complete faith that the Creator, blessed is His Name, is not physical and is not affected by physical phenomena, and that there is no comparison whatsoever to Him.

My Critique: This is a fair condensation of Rambam's point but would have been better without the last phrase about "no comparison" because that just repeats Rambam's previous point about Hashem's uniqueness and so obscures the progression of the argument that Rambam is building.

<u>The Yigdal Couplet:</u>
He has no semblance of a body nor is He corporeal. Nor has His holiness any comparison.

My Critique: Rambam never mentioned holiness. I can understand Yigdal using "holiness" to express "out of this world", meaning there is nothing in this universe like God. This idea takes it past the physicality expressed by Ani Ma'amin to probably exclude spirituality, too — nothing spiritual compares to God. I can agree with that, however, this goes beyond what Rambam said.

> **Rambam's third description of reality:** Denial of Hashem's physicality. Be clear that this Unity mentioned above is neither a body nor a physical

force. Actions of a body do not pertain to Hashem, either in essence or behavior.

Hence the sages of old avoided terms of composition and dissolution, saying, "above there is no sitting or standing...." (Talmud Chagigah 15a). The prophet said, "'To whom do you compare Me that I be equated,' says the Holy" (Is. 40:25), but were Hashem a body, Hashem would be comparable to [other] bodies.

Every reference of physical ways in the Holy Scriptures, such as walking or standing or sitting or speaking, or similar to it, is all by way of metaphor, as explained many times by the sages, "The Torah speaks in the language of people" (Talmud Berakhot 31b).

This third principle is indicated by, "for you did not see any image" (Deut. 4:15), meaning: you did not perceive Hashem as something with an image, because — as mentioned — Hashem is not a body nor the power within a body.

So far, **Rambam** has emphasized that Hashem loves to create and that all creation is a product of Hashem's imagination. Everything is really data; information packed together in different selections and sequences — forms and shapes, in our language — to present images. That leads to Rambam's next emphasis, Hashem's lack of an image.

I suspect you have an image in mind when Hashem is mentioned. The image is most likely a remnant from something you heard or saw when you were young. Whether it be a chariot of fire, a cloud-like form, an old, white-haired man, or a shining light, some image is bound to come to mind. The reason so many different images can come to mind is that there is no real image. Hashem has no body so there is nothing to see.

Don't Limit Hashem With An Image
Hashem the creator cannot have a body because Hashem was there before bodies were created. Some people may envision Hashem as a spirit in the form of a cloud but, realistically, clouds have bodies just like liquids. The outlines of a cloud or liquid body may be elastic — push down and it spreads out, push together and it piles up — not like our bodies, but bodies nonetheless.

Although difficult, we should try not to think of any image in reference to Hashem, which is why in earlier chapters, I used quantum mechanics and Google to describe Hashem. I hoped they would be much less likely to conjure an image for Hashem. The reason I want to avoid evoking a mental image for Hashem is that we tend to ascribe limitations to images if only to be able to draw the image in our minds. The harmful result will be a subconscious conviction that Hashem has limits. Consciously, we will continue to say Hashem is limitless, but subconsciously, we will be limiting the drawing (our concept) to stay within its lines.

God'll getcha?

Once we think of Hashem as a body, we think we can hide some unsavory detail from Hashem. A body has to occupy some space which means it has to be in that space and not another space. This suggests there is a space where that body is not. The harmful result of conceiving some kind of body for Hashem is to conclude that we could hide from Hashem in a space away from Hashem.

My late friend, Eugene Jerkowitz z"l, used to say "God'll getcha". I agreed with the conclusion but I used to criticize the premise. "God'll getcha" implies that there is a place one can hide but eventually Hashem will find it. I wanted Eugene to acknowledge that Hashem was constantly aware of our every action and location, as described above.

Eugene did acknowledge Hashem's awareness and maybe I was wrong to criticize "God'll getcha" because *Breishis* seems to imply it is true. In the story of Adam and Chava (Eve), they first eat the forbidden fruit, then become ashamed of their nakedness, then hide from

Hashem. When Hashem calls them out, they explain they were hiding their nakedness. From their awareness of nakedness, Hashem surmises they ate the forbidden fruit. So it does sound like Hashem had to find them and then figure out what they did.

That is the surface reading. However, as demonstrated in Chapter 1, the real story, reality itself, is hidden deep below the surface. A closer reading reveals that Hashem showed up as soon as they sinned. The timing suggests Hashem knew exactly where they were and what they had done.

Of course, Hashem knew because it was all happening in Hashem's mind, as it were. The reason for the "where are you?" and the ensuing dialogue was to give them a chance to confront and confess to their mistake. Although they did it with excuses, they did confess. In fact, their regret probably explains why they did not die that very day, as originally threatened.

Saying "sorry" resets the relationship. Even though Hashem threatened, "on the day you eat from the tree you will die", Hashem did not have to stay within the body of that threat. This is not mere wordplay; Hashem's lack of body means there are no limits on the options. Once we understand that we cannot hide from Hashem because Hashem has no body, we will also realize there is no advantage to hiding from Hashem.

Hashem is our creator and can create for us a new paradigm. That is how Hashem arranges everything to fit in. When Adam said "sorry" he was saying, "let me try again" to which Hashem replied, "ok, but I'll have to put you in different circumstances". Hashem created a setting other than the Garden of Eden — it is all in Hashem's mind. God'll getcha.

Where's the beef?

The above story illustrates how we can overcome the limits we perceive for ourselves. Adam and Chava thought they were doomed but they weren't; we often feel doomed but we, too, are not. The guarantee of this is the unlimited power of Hashem. That is not a new concept and most already accept it.

I want to expand it even more and show that there is no limit to Hashem's powers even when needing to break the very rules that Hashem does not want to break, such as the laws of Nature. I can prove this from a story that appears in Bamidbar, Chapter 11. It is ironic to find this story in Chapter 11 because, in America, Chapter 11 alludes to a bankruptcy situation and, in this story, we Jews display a bankruptcy of faith in Hashem.

After miraculously escaping Egyptian slavery and traveling through the wilderness for a while, our ancestors complain about the lack of meat to eat. They remember their fish and vegetable diet in Egypt and now they crave meat. This was unseemly of them because they weren't starving, there was wonderful food to eat. It was the Manna that miraculously fell from the sky every morning. Given this fact, it is understandable that Moshe complained to Hashem about the burden of leading such an ungrateful group of people, especially doing it alone. He was so depressed by the burden that he even prayed to Hashem for death, to be free of the burden.

This prayer must have caused a shock because Hashem responded right away. Hashem promised to bestow extra spirituality on a group of seventy elders with whom Moshe could share the burden. Not only that, Hashem promised to give immediate relief by providing meat for the people to eat. And not just once would Hashem provide the meat but every day for a month, until it was coming out of their noses. Hashem appears to have been insulted that they preferred meat to Manna, the food from Heaven.

Moshe's Surprise Question

So far, the frustrations felt by Moshe and Hashem in reaction to the complaints of the people are understandable. We can relate to the resulting plan of action. The next event, though, is quite surprising. Moshe questions Hashem. "Hashem", he asks, "what are You talking about?! I've got six hundred thousand men alone here (never mind the rest of the population), and You are promising to give them all meat? For a month? If You would slaughter all the sheep and cattle, would that be enough for them? Or if You gather all the fish in the sea, would that be enough for them?" To this, Hashem replies, "you think I will come up short-handed? Watch and see."

??What was Moshe thinking? Moshe was the miracle worker through whom all the ten plagues in Egypt were delivered. One of them was frogs underfoot everywhere. Another was a heavy infestation of wild animals. Even if Moshe was not aware that Hashem controls everything just by imagining it, he surely understood Hashem's complete control over the animal population. Moshe had a private audience with the Creator for forty days and nights on top of Mount Sinai. He must have become more intimate with Hashem's nature and power than we can ever fathom. How could he doubt Hashem's ability to provide meat?

When I have a question this perplexing, I often find the best way to answer it is by asking another question or two. Eventually, the questions answer each other. Here is what I asked. Why did the people want meat if they had heavenly Manna to eat? It must have tasted good and digested well otherwise it wouldn't have been considered "heavenly". And it was free for the taking. Why turn your back on a freebie? Oh, I see an answer coming already.

Most people are suspicious of freebies. They would rather work for a living. That way, they know they can take care of themselves. It makes one feel secure and self-sufficient. The Jewish people may have been slaves in Egypt but at least they earned their food with their work. This is the natural way we justify whatever pleasures we can eke out of our existence. "I earned this pleasure", we say to compliment ourselves.

The point of the Manna falling from Heaven was to teach the people that everything comes from Hashem. It only looks like you are earning it, but really it comes from Hashem. When the people complained they wanted meat, Moshe understood that it wasn't hunger that was bothering them but the loss of earning their own way. That is why he asked Hashem incredulously, "if You will make whatever miracle to give them all the sheep, cattle, or fish there are, how will that satisfy their desire to earn their way?"

Here's Why Hashem Planted The Question
Hashem's reply is amazing. "I don't need miracles to do what I want, I don't need superpowers. I have already built into nature all the powers I need to provide the messages I want to convey." In this non-miracle instance, Hashem brings a heavy migration of quail through the camp. They fly so low that everybody can grab as many as desired. The people tie them up and

make piles and piles of these birds, enough to last a month. So much more than they need that they get sick of it.

Migrations are quite normal. No miracle here. I can hear them saying: "It was my work that got me the piles of birds. Yes, it was unusual that they flew so low. Maybe it was the desert heat or a downward draft. I worked myself to a sweat in case the conditions would change suddenly."

The lesson is that even when we reject the solution Hashem had in mind for us, such as the Manna, Hashem will think — imagine — a new solution to engage us. Those twists and turns in the story that I spoke about earlier can come from either direction, us or Hashem!

This leads to astounding realizations for ourselves. Hashem is constantly imagining new scenarios for us. There will always be challenges motivating us to find solutions. Think of before the invention of the telephone in the latter half of the 1800s. How many people could have imagined how profoundly life would change? Even after it arrived, who could have guessed the endless apps that a smartphone would provide? All through the ages, there have been wise men, sometimes the wisest of the wise, who have proclaimed, "now, we have invented everything, there is nothing else to develop".

They continually underestimate Hashem's imagination. No matter. That is part of the plan.

On the other hand, we could invent our own direction. There is no limit. Suppose, instead of all the energy poured into telecommunications, we had poured it in a different direction, say to promote the use of a universal language that would unite people. Think of the changes to society that could have been brought about. Or into underground cities that wouldn't require so much energy to maintain a comfortable temperature year-round? Think of the implications for so many industries that would have entailed. Or what other inventions might we have developed and will develop?

Have we not by now learned that we have unlimited potential? It is all because Hashem has built-in unlimited development. Perhaps, the examples I proposed above are unlikely or unnecessary. Then consider instead the many heroic responses by people who did not start as heroes but rose to become one. There are innumerable examples that prove the potential. These people were inspired by a need and rose to the occasion. Some even rose to fame. True, some didn't, but each changed every life they touched. We all know or have heard of such individuals. It would not have been likely that they succeeded — they would be the first to admit — had Hashem not built into the system non-miracle miracles.

Answer to: Why Can't We See Hashem? We cannot see Hashem because there is no body to see. No lines can draw Hashem's limits. The reason we have to know this is to realize, as products of Hashem's mind, we also have no limits. Certainly not the limits we perceive. Hashem re-draws those lines all the time, as we push at them. Based on human progress to date, one might even say that Hashem hopes we push at those lines to have good reason to redraw them. Remember, Hashem likes to create.

4 - What's My Choice If Hashem Knows The Future?

<u>The Familiar Ani Ma'amin</u>: I believe with complete faith that the Creator, blessed is His Name, is the very first and the very last.

My Critique: Many interpret this statement of Rambam as being about Hashem's Eternity which is why the Ani Ma'amin uses the phrase "very first and very last". Rambam certainly agrees Hashem is timeless, but I don't think that is what he meant here. All Rambam said was that Hashem was preexisting, meaning first. Rambam never mentioned last. Emphasizing Hashem was first is a statement about sequence, not timelessness.

<u>The Yigdal Couplet</u>:
He preceded every being that was created —
the First, and nothing precedes His precedence.

My Critique: Finally, a faithful rendition of Rambam's point! This allows me to focus on how this point advances the argument.

> **Rambam's fourth description of reality:** Be clear about preexistence. This Unity that we mentioned is absolutely preexisting, and no other existing thing besides Him existed before Him.

The proofs to this in the Holy Scriptures are many. This fourth principle is indicated by, "The abode of the preexisting Hashem" (Deut. 33:27).

Rambam continues describing Hashem in a way that leads us to understand our reality. Those that understand this as a statement about Hashem's timelessness have to deal with a famous quandary — a seemingly unanswerable contradiction — but don't worry, I have a novel solution.

Modern science has determined that time is part of the space-time continuum. Some use this to claim Hashem is timeless, as follows. If time is a creation just like space, energy, and matter, then Hashem cannot be confined by time because Hashem created time. This fact leads us to conclude that Hashem knows the future because Hashem is outside time.

Others make the same conclusion from the opposite direction. If Hashem did not know the future, then Hashem would not be all-knowing and all-powerful, an unacceptable limitation. Since Hashem must know the future, Hashem must be outside of time.

Hashem's Omniscience vs. Free Choice
The primary problem with this conclusion, from whatever direction it is derived, is its contradiction to free choice. If

Hashem knows what we will choose before we choose it, then we are <u>not</u> free to choose otherwise. Conversely, if we are free to choose differently, then Hashem will <u>not</u> have known our future choice and something is missing in Hashem's omniscience.

Most people, especially religious ones, insist we have free choice. Otherwise, we are governed by unseen forces and should not be held accountable — a religiously unacceptable position. On the other hand, religious people insist that Hashem knows everything, even the future. The quandary is famous and unavoidable.

One answer offered to solve this quandary is to separate the mere knowledge of an act from control over that act. Just like my knowledge of what happened in the past does not affect that event — it transpired in the way it did whether I ever learned of it or not — so too, if I know of a future event, I need not affect that event, it will transpire whether I know of it or not.

The words work but not the thought. As soon as I know of a past event, I can react to that event. If Hashem knows of a future event, Hashem must be able to react right away, including stopping it. That takes away my free choice — an unacceptable conclusion.

That is one reason I do not like the preceding answer. Another reason is that Rambam (see: Mishneh Torah, Laws of Repentance, Ch. 5:5), raises the question and assures us there is an answer but it is too deep to present on paper. But I was able to write out the answer proposed above without too much difficulty; knowledge of an act is separate from control over that act — there it is. That is why I assume he didn't like this answer any more than I did and it was not the one he had in mind.

I stand in awe of Rambam's wisdom. The more I read him and analyze his choice of words, the more I realize how consistently well he plumbed the depths of reality and presented it with unassailable precision. Nevertheless, I dare to present below a solution to the conundrum that he left unsolved — undoubtedly not the one he had in mind. I dare do this <u>not</u> because I understand it better than him — I would never be so presumptuous. I dare because I and my audience have the advantage of modern discoveries that Rambam did not. These provide new insights that lead to new models of expression that I can use to offer a new perspective.

Two Computer Systems Unveil How Hashem Thinks
Blondie24 is the name of a computer program that was designed in 1999 to play checkers. (Checkers is a game played on the same board as Chess, but with simpler pieces and rules.)

Blondie24's design included a model of evolution, as follows. The program was able to clone itself with some random variations and then play a game against its clone. Whichever version lost the game was erased and the victorious version was cloned again with new random variations, and the process repeated.

Given the rapid speed at which machines compute, it was possible to clone through many, many "generations" in short order. The victorious versions kept getting better over the generations. Eventually, a version became so adept at the game of checkers that it was able to defeat people with a master's level of skill.

Blondie24 learned the way we learn, by trial and error. The more times we try, the better we become.

Chinook was also a computer program designed to play checkers. Its "brains" were a database of all the possible moves in a checkers game. That number is so huge (5×10^{20}) that it took years for many computers working 24/7 to compile all those moves. Nevertheless, the number is finite, the list comes to an end.

When Chinook plays, for every move its opponent makes, Chinook selects from the entire population of possible future moves the one move most likely to lead to a win. Chinook does not know which moves its opponent will choose in the future. It doesn't have to.

Instead, it looks at all possible futures and selects the move that most likely leads to a win. Instead of a chance, it takes a thoughtful aim. Chinook doesn't know the exact future but it knows all possible futures.

While Blondie24 is a model of how people think, Chinook may be a model of how Hashem thinks.

Hashem, being first, created all possible futures. Having created them, Hashem knows them. In order to govern the world, Hashem need not know what any particular person will choose. Hashem needs only to know all the choices the particular person can make and what moves to make in reply.

This capability hinges on the fact that Hashem was first. Being first, nothing else could have assembled those choices except Hashem. I propose this is what Rambam meant when he said Hashem was preexisting.

A Personal Relationship With Hashem
This model of Hashem's knowledge removes the contradiction between Hashem's foreknowledge and free will. But, for me, the model does much more than that. It provides me with a personal relationship with Hashem. Before the model, my free choice was immaterial to Hashem. Since my choices were already known, whatever reactions from Hashem they

demanded were already set in place. That model envisioned Hashem as a pre-programmed automaton.

True, my awareness of those reactions was missing and, admittedly, it is interesting to see how my life unfolds. But not interesting enough to keep me passionate about it. I was passionate in my younger days when I did not yet have the experience of "that is the way it goes". But now I have such experience and it dulls my passion for life. "That is the way it goes" is a tired refrain common to seniors. It eviscerates life with boredom.

However, now I realize that my actual choices are not pre-known; now I can sense Hashem's personal interest. Hashem is curious to see how I turn out and what to do about it. Hashem is even actively involved in managing me in accordance with how everybody else is turning out. Right up to the last minute.

According to the concept that I introduced in Chapter 2 of quantum mechanical twists and turns in the story we create, we may even be able to introduce new choices that were not pre-known and not even pre-conceived. In this scenario, as God's subconscious, we create a new choice to add to existence. *ALoHYM* then considers whether to allow such a new element, which will probably depend on what new counter moves will also have to be added to assure a winning game. (In this way, Hashem's pre-existence continues to exert control over what else comes into existence.) If it is allowed, then we act it out, adding to the universe. No wonder Hashem's design includes an expanding universe — it is not only the Big Bang expanding it—it is also expanding to accommodate our creative thoughts.

I am awed by the number of reactions Hashem can muster to guide my life. I am eager to select a positive choice because it will make a difference, not only to myself but also to everyone else. Hashem is taking it all into account. Granted, the difference I make to the overall scheme of things might be too small for me to detect. Still, the difference I make is to Hashem, a Being beyond measure, so that is quite an accomplishment.

Hashem Must Be Logical

If Hashem is waiting for my choices, is Hashem still timeless? Yes, at least in the sense that Hashem is not subject to the ravages of time. Hashem did not start younger and less capable nor does Hashem grow old or decay. Hashem does not change in essence. I have no problem saying that because it is not illogical. There are things in our experience that do not change. Rocks and the sun used to be the quoted examples of things that do not change. Perhaps these aren't good examples any longer because science has discovered changes in them, such as radioactive decay in rocks and flare-ups in the sun.

If that be argued, I present the fact of 1 + 1 = 2. That doesn't change. If it did change, it would be illogical, beyond our capacity to relate. Not being able to relate to a rule means there is no rule. For that very reason, I assert that Hashem must be logical because, if not, we cannot relate — what would be the point? — we might as well erase the concept of Hashem. (Comparing God to the rule 1+1=2 is particularly appropriate because, like any rule, God is not physical, as previously discussed.)

Having asserted that Hashem must be logical, let me brush aside an old diatribe. "Can Hashem make a rock he cannot lift? If yes, then he is not all-powerful. If not, then he lacks the power to make such a rock."

I will answer in two ways. First, accept that Hashem is not all-powerful by that definition. So what? The question assumes a definition of power that is unnecessary — ignore it. (Incidentally, by using the pronoun "he", the question also ascribes a male identity to Hashem — something I have carefully avoided as another unnecessary definition.) Second, realize the question is inherently illogical by restating it. "Can an all-powerful being make something not subject to its power?" That is the same as asking "can a yes be a no?" It is illogical to ask.

Back to timeless Hashem. I agree that Hashem is not subject to the ravages of time. That doesn't necessarily mean that Hashem is not subject to logical sequence. Einstein posited that time passes at different rates depending on gravity and speed; subsequent experiments have proven it. Hashem created those rates so they can't govern Hashem. In that sense, Hashem is timeless. But not timeless in another sense, the sense of one o'clock coming before two o'clock.

Logic dictates that certain things must happen in sequence. For example, flour and water must come together before a dough can be formed. Several variables can change. The water may come first or last and the amounts of water and flour could vary, and so on, but the dough cannot form without the prerequisites of flour and water. When this sequence occurs, Hashem calls it bread. If the bread appears without flour and water, Hashem calls it Manna, not dough or bread because it didn't follow the sequence.

Proof that Hashem is subject to sequence can be found in the very first word of the Torah which translates as "in the beginning". With the first word of the Torah, Hashem introduced sequence into the universe, making it part of our logic — prerequisites must come first. Hashem must comply else why introduce the idea. Since Hashem has to wait for a sequence to end, Hashem has to wait to see how I turn out.

Answer to: What Choice Do I Have If Hashem Knows The Future? Since nothing preceded Hashem, there were no pre-existing rules or mindsets that Hashem had to follow when creating. The idea, the design, the execution are all the products of Hashem's mind. Therefore, it all fits in, it all serves the overall purpose of the one Creator. Nobody is an afterthought or a begrudged inclusion. This thought is the first building block of our self-image.

The second building block of our self-image is that our decisions matter, they change things. Hashem arranged all the future possibilities as "moves" and "countermoves". Sometimes, we can even add more possibilities similar to a character in a story that suddenly inspires the storyteller to add a new twist to the plot. In any case, our choice between "moves" is the creation we make. Making that choice prompts Hashem to a different set of "countermoves". Calling that choice a creation leads us to Rambam's next description of reality.

5 - What's In It For Hashem?

<u>The Familiar Ani Ma'amin</u>: I believe with complete faith that the Creator, blessed is His Name—to Him alone is it proper to pray and it is not proper to pray to any other.

My Critique: This concisely reflects the view of most commentaries who interpret Rambam's statement as one about prayer. I approach Rambam's statement from a very different angle that eventually leads back to prayer but not as the main thought.

<u>The Yigdal Couplet</u>:
Behold! He is Master of the universe to every creature,
He demonstrates His greatness and His sovereignty.

My Critique: Whereas Rambam articulated the service part of a master-servant relationship, this couplet describes the mastery part. This obscures Rambam's main message.

Rambam's fifth description of reality: Hashem is the One that it is fitting to serve, to exalt, to make Hashem's greatness known, and to perform Hashem's mitzvah instructions.

Do not do this to lower creatures such as the angels, the stars, the spheres, the elements, and what is composed of them. They are all programmed by Hashem; there is no judgment or free choice in their actions.

Thus, do not use them as intermediaries to get closer to Hashem. Rather, to Hashem alone should we direct our thoughts, leaving everything else aside.

This fifth principle is that idolatry is prohibited, as admonished throughout the Torah.

I must warn you about this chapter because, here, I probably make my most radical departure from the way most others understand this **Rambam**. This warning applies to two types of readers. If you never studied these statements of Rambam before, I warn you not to think less of him if I say something unacceptable. That fault would be mine, not Rambam's. If you have read Rambam's statements elsewhere, I warn you to read the following carefully. It will not conform to what you thought, and it may persuade you to think differently.

Most understand Rambam here to be requiring prayer because he opened with the word "serve", a code word for prayer. The code comes from the following teaching.

A Torah verse says "...serve Hashem with all your heart and soul..." (Deut. 11:13) about which the sages ask "what is the service of the heart?" They answer "prayer is service of the heart" as derived from another verse, "...don't follow your heart..." (Num. 15:39). I understand the connection between these ideas is as follows.

Our hearts want a lot of things. We know that some of those desires lead us astray. For those things, we dare not ask Hashem. Instead, we keep them hidden in our hearts until an opportunity arrives, then we pounce. But there are some things our hearts want about which Hashem would approve. For those things, we do turn to Hashem in prayer. That means that before expressing our prayers, we have refined our list of heartfelt desires in consideration of what Hashem would like to hear. That is a service of the heart and that is how "serve" came to be a code word for "prayer".

We pray to Hashem to get the things we want. Before asking anybody for anything, it is advisable to assume confidence in the request being granted. That makes the benefactor reluctant to disappoint the petitioner. For this reason, we praise Hashem before asking for anything, to remind ourselves to be confident of getting what we want. Pray with confidence.

After we pray, we thank Hashem even though we have not yet been answered. The reason is to remind ourselves to be grateful for past favors. Any benefactor who sees that we appreciate past favors is more motivated to satisfy a new request. But if past favors have not been appreciated, there is much less incentive to do a new favor. That goes for everyone who might help us. That is why it goes for Hashem, too, who wants us to help each other. Our parents train us the same way—say please and thank you.

The above explains how the acts of praising Hashem and thanking Hashem both merge with the act of asking Hashem to form a proper prayer. It also explains why most other commentaries interpreted as prayer the opening words of Rambam: "serve" (pray to Hashem for what we want), "exalt" (praise Hashem), and "make greatness known" (publicize our appreciation).

However, prayer does not adequately cover Rambam's last phrase, "perform Hashem's mitzvah instructions". Prayer is just one of 613 mitzvah instructions so why mention all mitzvahs when trying to single out prayer?

Indeed, why is prayer singled out by Rambam for inclusion in this list? Most call Rambam's list the fundamentals of the faith. I call it descriptions of reality. In either case, why consider prayer more fundamental than other mitzvah instructions such as kosher, Shabbos, loving one's fellow?

Another problem with prayer is that it does not fit the pattern of these thirteen statements. Every religion has to answer three questions. Who should you worship? From where did you learn that? What happens if you do and if you don't? Rambam's first four points of the thirteen describe who we worship, his four points from 6-9 demonstrate how we learned to do that, and his last four points (10-13) elaborate on the consequences, as I shall present. Where does prayer fit in?

My answer to the above is to add a new question. Not only does Rambam address the three questions above, he also addresses: Why did Hashem do all this? Or, to put it more colloquially, What's in it for Hashem? This question is the real subject of this, his fifth point.

What's In It For Hashem?

A recap of my presentation thus far will set up my answer to this question:

1. Hashem loves to create, in ever-increasing levels of sophistication, from the billions of inert stars, up to the myriad forms of vegetation, up to diverse life forms such as insects, animals, birds, and sea life, and finally to sentient humans.
2. Hashem created all this out of nothing but willpower, a mind.
3. Hashem has no body which means no limits, unlimited power. There is no limit to what empowers us.

4. Hashem knows all scenarios that could happen but does not control them. Why not? Apparently, out of interest to learn what choices we make and what reactions would best suit our potential.

Given that Hashem loves to create, what is the highest form of life that Hashem could create? The answer should be, as *Breishis* reports, something in the image of the Creator. How are we in the image of Hashem? The answer is, we have free will with which to create.

What do we create? Don't answer "babies". Animals make babies. Even plants make babies through their seeds. But, animals and plants are not in Hashem's image. In what way do we qualify for this exalted description?

The answer is, we create just like Hashem creates, with our minds. Relationships, ideas, concepts, solutions to problems (that probably we created), arts, music, strategies, even games. All these may have physical expression but still exist beforehand, in our minds. They start from our minds.

We create with our minds just like the Creator created us with a mind. We are the most sophisticated form of creation that Hashem could make because we are a creature that itself could create. Out of nothing more than our minds. We are Hashem's creative ability deployed to the max.

Serving Hashem's Purpose

Following this reasoning, I suggest Rambam's opening of serving Hashem did not mean prayer, it meant serving Hashem's purpose of having more data to correlate. The best thing for an active mind—which is what Hashem is—is more things to think about. To serve Hashem's purpose, we should create. Create relationships, ideas, concepts, solutions, arts, music, strategies, and even games, as many as we can, as often as we can.

Hashem could hardly wait for us to do this. The first Torah mitzvah instruction is to be fruitful and multiply—have babies. The main reason is not to populate the world. That will come only after quite a while. However, we will immediately become busy forming new relationships with the baby, the youth, the teenager, the heir, plus with our spouse—who changes at each stage, too. Baby will also change our relationships with our parents as we begin to understand them better and change our relationships with those who provide a community for Baby. We will create plans for the future. All the foregoing from just one baby. Wait till you try two!

There are countless other opportunities and reasons to create. Hashem certainly knows how to design it so that we will create.

Following his opening of serving Hashem, Rambam next suggests we exalt Hashem. This follows naturally. By praising Hashem we come to admire Hashem's achievement. Out of admiration, we mimic the activity because we also want to be admired, to be praised. Intuitively, women accomplish this by nurturing a family.

Men also have a natural impulse to create something of their own, something in which they can take pride and receive praise. It might be the product they make, the service they perform, or just the telling of a story they made up. Or even just the organization of a room, a shop. It is their creation. They take pride in it. Meanwhile, its composition glorifies Hashem because it fulfills Hashem's purpose, to create a being that itself can create out of nothing external, using only its mind.

Hashem's glory does not rely on the size of the creation or even its intricacy because those are physical qualities and Hashem is not physical. Rather, Hashem's glory will depend on the creativity demonstrated with the resources available.

Rambam next suggests we make Hashem's greatness known. Publicizing Hashem's praise has a domino effect because it encourages others to be creative. We need not fear that their creativity will hamper ours because, as established earlier, Hashem has no body, no limits. There is an unlimited amount Hashem can allow us to create in our minds. In this respect, we emulate the image of Hashem.

However, we are unlike Hashem in one aspect. Hashem knows all the future results of the moves we make, but we don't. We make lots of mistakes, many of which can destroy us, especially in a social or emotional sense. That is why Rambam continues his point by cautioning us to follow Hashem's mitzvahs. These Torah behaviors guide us away from creating mistakes with our minds such as bad relationships, bad ideas, weapons, pollution, pornography, substance abuse, etc.

We can't easily detect how these Torah behaviors protect us socially and emotionally but then neither can we detect how vaccines administered by our doctors protect us from falling ill.

That is a good analogy. We should treat each mitzvah as if it were a vaccination against a spiritually harmful virus. However, a few mitzvahs are not enough because our soul is even more complicated than our virus-susceptible body. So, just like a medical vaccine can fail sometimes, presumably because our bodies are weak in other areas (eg. co-morbidities), our everyday

Torah behaviors can fail to always protect. They can fail when we have weakened our souls in other areas. That is why there are so many mitzvah instructions—to protect and nourish the complexities of our soul.

Rambam Next Warns About Idols

Instinctively, we create but oftentimes we do it badly. How do we normally respond to the destructive nature of our creations? We tend to double down. Rather than admit an error, especially one emanating from a subconscious desire, we defend it—even to the point of championing it. You might say, we worship it. That is why, after exhorting us to protect ourselves with as many mitzvah instructions as we can, Rambam warns us not to worship the errors we champion—don't make them idols. Do not worship the things you create, he says.

Do you realize how we become so entranced with the satisfying aspect of what we create that we wind up believing it is our only option? The following example could be applied to any number of scenarios. A person seeks relief from a frustrating day at work by watching a two-hour-long TV program. It works that night to calm his nerves, so the person schedules two hours of TV the next night and then the next. Meanwhile, the problem at work disappears or he adjusts to it. The days stop being frustrating and he no longer needs a diversion. But he continues the ritual, in blind obedience to the comfort it once offered. Two hours every night that might have been spousal time or parenting time or learning time become permanently lost to an idolized routine. The star of our story has become an idol worshiper!

If the star of our story never questions the routine, he may start praying to it. How do you pray to such an idol? "I hope there is a good program on tonight" or "I sure hope I can celebrate my team's win tonight." Isn't "I hope" the same as "I pray"? Isn't it true that many of the things we celebrate such as sports and celebrities have no actual bearing on the lives we lead? Isn't it also true that many of the things we wish for are just that, wishful thoughts, that will transpire one way or the other, unaffected by our hopes and wishes? Wishing them to be, or praying for them, or to them is absurd. But this is what we do! The lesson is, we should not imagine ourselves any more sophisticated than those ancestors who prayed to idols.

Back To Prayer
Mentioning prayer takes me back to where I started. Maybe Rambam's point here is about prayer after all but in a more roundabout way. Our freedom to create allows us to create mistakes for ourselves which we often do. Some mistakes are so wrong-headed that they limit our future. In the process of trying to break through these limitations, we often grasp desperately at straws rather than correct our wrong-headedness. That is just another

way of saying we pray to false idols. Just as we know the straws we grasp will break and fail us, we ought to realize that these false ideas will not work either. No sense in hoping they will, no sense in praying to them.

Get real. Don't lose sight of unlimited Hashem! Ask Hashem for help, pray for the wisdom of knowing what to do. Hashem is the guarantee we can break through the limits we have created for ourselves.

Hashem creates us by focusing a mind on us. It only makes sense that we can enhance ourselves, our creative ability, by focusing our mind back on Hashem; it is like completing an electricity-like circuit. We make Hashem grow in creative reputation, Hashem makes us grow in creative ability.

Answer to: What's In It For Hashem? Humans enable Hashem to create more and better because we can create like Hashem creates, with our minds. This represents a new level of sophistication in Hashem's creation—even Hashem's creations now create creations—giving Hashem something new to oversee and empower. From our perspective, it seems Hashem enjoys matching our creativity with realisitic opportunities to create.

I must hasten to caution, Hashem is not of this world and is really beyond our imagination. Rambam, himself, said this. Nevertheless, he spent some time describing Hashem as best as he could. These efforts display Rambam's conviction that a deeper understanding of Hashem enables us to think more creatively. I share that conviction of Rambam's which is why I am proposing new descriptions of our relationship to and with Hashem.

6 - How Does Hashem Talk To Us?

<u>The Familiar Ani Ma'amin</u>: I believe with complete faith that all the words of the prophets are true.

My Critique: I find this rendition of Rambam's point difficult to accept because there have been false prophets whose words were not true. If you will answer that they were not real prophets then belief in the truth of prophetic words relies on circular reasoning.

<u>The Yigdal Couplet</u>:
He granted His flow of prophecy
to His treasured, splendid people.

My Critique: This is better because it simply acknowledges the idea of prophecy, some of which was granted to the Jewish people.

Rambam's sixth description of reality: Prophecy: everyone should know that among the human species, there are those who naturally tend towards highly elevated character traits and great wholeness and whose souls become fit to receive the pure intellectual form. Eventually, their human intellect clings to the Active Intellect and receives a profound

---

emanation. These are the prophets and this is the understanding of prophecy.

The full elucidation of this principle is very lengthy but it is not our purpose to demonstrate all of its paradigms and elucidate the nature of its attainment as this would require a full exposition on wisdom. I only mention it in passing; the verses of the Torah testify to the prophecy of many prophets.

Rambam, in the previous step, cautioned us to follow Hashem's mitzvah instructions; they are designed to keep us away from negative creations such as adversarial relationships, wanton conduct, false goals, and other mistakes. But how did we get these mitzvah instructions? Rambam now tells us about prophets, our source of those instructions; how to recognize them, and what to expect from them.

Born Or Bred

Note the path Rambam takes to describe it. He explains that some people display early on a very refined character, an elevated soul, and a probing intellect. These qualities reveal inborn talents that they have exercised and developed over time. Such people can further develop themselves to reach extraordinary spiritual clarity. Eventually, they might be granted prophecy at which point the person will hear Hashem speaking to them supernaturally. Prophecy is supernatural wisdom.

Supernatural wisdom? Most will agree that it has been many ages since prophecy of this type has been granted. Already when Rambam lived, prophecy had been absent for over a thousand years. This made me wonder why Rambam felt it so important to include prophecy as a separate point — he could have rolled it into his upcoming points about the Torah conveyed by prophets.

Asking that question led me to recognize that Rambam had not just identified prophecy; he had described the process of developing into a prophet. Contemplating that process, I realized that the same description applies to every other human talent. Rambam has used prophecy as a template to describe how Hashem sprinkles the creative urge among us.

We find that, in our world and in every age, people are born with a gift of one kind or another. Some are good with their hands, some are musical or artistic or athletic. Some are charismatic. In every human endeavor, some people excel naturally in one or more ways, physically, mentally, and/or emotionally. These are the ones who go on to develop the things we need.

What are the things we need? Occasionally, they are the things that bring a smile to our faces. But usually, they are the things that remove pain and discomfort. It is just these pains and discomforts that finally motivate someone to overcome them.

Earlier, we determined that Hashem created us so that we could create, in imitation of Hashem. "Could create" was not enough, Hashem had to make sure we would create. That is why Hashem provides problems that challenge or pain us—to motivate us to create solutions. Without the problems, we tend to coast complacently and do nothing.

Stars and Superstars
From the dawn of civilization, different skills were needed to secure water sources, food supplies, shelters, communication tools, systems for organizing and governing ourselves, and so on. The Torah never records any practical advice from Hashem in these matters. Instead, the dispersal of different skills and talents constituted silent advice—figure it out and solve your problem. That is equivalent to: "create a solution".

Problems prod each person to develop their skills and maybe even become a star, the go-to guy in their community. Some problem solvers become superstars through a combination of their determination and a crowning inspiration, probably a gift from Hashem.

A songwriter finally links the perfect combination of words to a melody that will inspire generations. An artist mixes the right colors that capture the soul of the object and stirs the mind of the observer. An athlete synchronizes a jump and a twist into a moment of grace that others wish to imitate.

Hashem will not do our work for us because the whole idea was for us to create, on our own. That is Hashem's delight.

To encourage creativity, Hashem spreads talents among a wide variety of people so that they can become a star at what they do. In support of their efforts, Hashem may grace a person with unusual success to motivate all those who are not yet trying to start trying: "join the crowd, already!" And to all those already trying, to try harder: "you too can excel!"

All In The Family

The drive to create is even more common with regard to family relationships. So common, it is automatic. Everybody comes from a family and every family operates differently. Why? Because there are variables unique to each family, a whole list of them.

Start your list with the first unique feature of a face. Add the uniqueness science has uncovered about each person, such as fingerprints and DNA. They confirm all the other personal peculiarities your common sense detects among individuals—pretty or plain, confident or shy, bold or timid, athletic or flat-footed, tall, fat, intelligent, etc.

Continue the list with the uniqueness of a family which is a group of unique persons assembled by accident. (Actually by Hashem, but since we didn't choose the personalities to be included, from our perspective it was an accident.) Each of us struggles to coordinate our distinct talents and personalities with the other family members. Can you still remember the struggles of your youth? There was no template for us to follow. The coordination strategies we each developed for our circumstances were unique, a new creation, as Hashem intended.

Notwithstanding Hashem's intention, these relationships can go off in the wrong direction, as we well know, but learn too late.

In physical areas of creativity, the choices can also go off in the wrong direction, but there is a feedback loop. For example, when one tries to build a better mousetrap, the target audience will react. If the product works they will offer rewards in the form of money or praise. If it doesn't, they will criticize it —too hard to use, too expensive, etc. Such feedback teaches the product creator how to improve it.

In family matters, there is no such feedback loop. The relationships start forming in a way that satisfies our immediate needs. Future results cannot be predicted so they are not considered. Only after the fact do family leaders learn that they may have been too aggressive, too lazy, too suppressive, too assertive and so on. What is then needed is for family members to slowly create solutions, workarounds, or sensitivities to these missteps. Again, a challenge to create.

Gather all the family relationships together and you get Society, where relationships become even more complex. These complicated relationships are known as business models, governing ideas, diplomatic strategies, artistic fashions, music genres, and even games. We know from history and current experience that these relationships demand even greater creativity. A superstar is needed because Society will not know for a long time, if ever, the exact repercussions of their behavior choices.

Perfect Relationships Are Hard To Create
For these reasons, Hashem used to provide prophets who were capable of guiding others in best behavior practices. These prophets were self-made stars who acquired a superstar type of wisdom and spirituality that

came from Hashem's grace. That superstar stature was designed to gain attention; then they could convince others how to build a society, teach them a sense of purpose (same as a sense of holiness), and model for them a connection with the creator.

Two questions arise. First, why didn't Hashem provide everybody with the talent to become a prophet? The answer is simple. Hashem didn't set everybody up to become a prophet (or any other kind of superstar) because that diminishes the range of creativity possible. Diversity not only displays Hashem's delight in creating, it also leads to more creativity from us. Different talents and varying degrees of competency within each talent provide room for each person to create their own achievement.

Take music for example. One person is born with perfect pitch and, driven by such talent, will concentrate on tuning the instruments properly, selecting the best sound mix, and harmonizing the musicians. An orchestra is created.

Another person is born without a perfect pitch. It never enters their head to be so technically precise about their music. Instead, that person composes a beat to fit the words that cry out his longing. A haunting melody is created.

Second question, why did Hashem stop providing prophets? The same sort of answer as above could be proposed. Just like different competencies allow a broader range of creative solutions, so too do different environments, different cultures, and even different personality mixes. For example, while a prophet would assist Group A to create an impregnable connection with Hashem, a non-prophet would assist Group B to create a different connection, a weaker one, one not impregnable but the best possible, under the circumstances. That would be their particular achievement, treasured all the more for the greater struggle needed to make it possible. Any connection with Hashem completes a unique circuit, an electricity-like circuit of our life force, namely, Hashem's response to our creative choices.

Another answer may be more historically correct. Hashem stopped providing prophets because the position got filled by charlatans. Everybody dreams of being a superstar, but few are able to qualify. Even fewer are willing to do the work required. There is a large temptation to fake it. In the realm of physical creation, the public is not so easily deceived. They quickly learn what works and what doesn't. But, in the realm of spirituality, the public is easily deceived because they don't want to do the work either.

There are plenty of stories of real prophets who were unable to inspire change in the behavior of their countrymen. Despite their superstardom, other charismatic characters were more successful leaders because they gave the people what they wanted, something easy. Unfortunately, people who follow charisma, instead of the reality that a prophet offers, wind up self-destructing. By removing prophecy, Hashem replaced this potential for self-destruction with the more modest goal of a weaker connection with Hashem, but one more likely to germinate.

Answer to: How Does Hashem Talk To Us? Prophecy teaches us about the full range of human potential. Hashem gives us problems, not answers, but provides teachers to help us create answers ourselves. Prophets were the supply teachers for the spiritual issues that arose.

Reality hasn't changed. Just like we don't need a new mathematician to discover the axioms of geometry, so too, we don't need new prophets to uncover spiritual guidance that has already been transmitted. In the next three points, Rambam describes how that was accomplished.

7 - Why Moshe Our Teacher, Not Our Prophet?

The Familiar Ani Ma'amin: I believe with complete faith that the prophecy of Moshe, our teacher, peace upon him, was true, and that he was the father of the prophets—both those who preceded him and those who followed him.

My Critique: Since the previous Ani ma'amin already asserted that all prophets were true, it was needless and confusing, to repeat here that Moshe's prophecy was true. The rest of this Ani ma'amin tries to reflect the effort Rambam made to describe Moshe as the greatest prophet, ever. (Rambam used more words for this statement than for any of the others.)

The Yigdal Couplet:
In Israel, none like Moshe arose again –
a prophet who perceived His vision clearly.

My Critique: The extra word "again" may have been inserted to satisfy those who argue that forefather Avraham was greater than Moshe, especially since he started with less than Moshe did.

The phrase "in Israel" allows for greater prophets outside Israel. Indeed, some sources suggest Bilaam, a non-Jew, was a greater prophet than Moshe. Even if this were true, it does not undermine Rambam's argument because Bilaam left no record of his prophecies. We only know of them from Moshe's record in the Torah.

Rambam's seventh description of reality: Moshe, our teacher, was the father of all prophets before and after him, meaning, all are below his level of prophecy. He was chosen to grasp more of Hashem's knowledge than any man who lived or ever will live. He reached an elevation equal to the level of angels, as if in their domain. No barrier did he not pierce, no physical impediment hindered him and no defect—large or small—afflicted him. All physical constraints and perceptions disappeared from him; arousals and desires were removed from him; he retained only intellect. One way of describing this is that he would speak with Hashem without an angelic intermediary.

I desired to unlock and elucidate this amazing matter from the verses of the Torah, including the meaning of "Mouth to mouth" (Num.12:8) and so on. However, I saw that it would require too many proofs prefaced by many propositions, introductions, and parables. First, I would have to elucidate the meaning of angels and their levels from the Creator, Hashem. Then, I would have to elucidate the [nature of the] soul and all of its powers. I would need to expound on the terms that the prophets used to describe the Creator and the angels. To just briefly outline it, a hundred pages would not suffice. Therefore, I will leave it for another work, whether in the book of homilies that I intend to write or in the books of prophecy with which I am involved or in a separate book that I will write to elucidate these principles.

Instead, I will focus on this seventh principle and explain how the prophecy of Moshe, our teacher is distinct from the prophecy of all [other] prophets in four ways:

The first one is that all other prophets were only spoken to by Hashem through an intermediary. But Moshe was without an intermediary, as it states, "Mouth to mouth will I speak to him."

The second distinction is that any [other] prophet would not get prophecy except when he was sleeping—as it is stated in many places, "in a dream at night," "in an apparition at night", etc.—or during the day after falling into a trance in such a way that all of his feelings disappear from him and his [faculty of] thought becomes [fully] available, like in a dream. This is called an apparition or a vision, as stated, "the vision of Hashem." However, the [divine] speech would come to Moshe during the day while he was standing between the two cherubs (of the tabernacle), as Hashem testified, "I will meet you there"

(Ex.25:22); see also Num.12:6-8: "if you will have prophecies, etc. Not so is my servant, Moshe [...] Mouth to mouth I will speak to him, etc."

The third distinction is that when a prophecy comes to [another] prophet—even though it is in a vision and through an angel—nevertheless, his powers weaken and his frame shrinks and a very great fear comes upon him; [so much so] that his spirit almost leaves him, as it is stated in Daniel 10:8-16, when [the angel,] Gavriel spoke with him, he said, "there remained no strength in me and my expression changed upon me to destruction and I retained no strength," and he said, "I was asleep on my face and my face was to the ground," and he said, "my pains have turned upon me." But Moshe was not like this; the [divine] word would come upon him without fear and trembling in any way; as it is stated (Ex.33:11), "the Lord would speak to Moshe, face to face, as a man would speak to his fellow"; which is to say, just like the speech of his friend does not cause trembling to a person, so [too] Moshe would not tremble from the [divine] word, even though he was face to face. This is due to the strength of his intellect's cleaving [to Hashem], as I have mentioned.

The fourth distinction is that the spirit of prophecy did not rest upon all of the [other] prophets whenever they wanted, but only when Hashem wanted. Indeed, a prophet might remain for days or years and not receive a prophecy. He would plead with the Creator, Hashem, to inform him about something and then have to wait for days or months until he prophesied. He might never get informed. Some would prepare themselves and purify their thoughts—as Elisha did, "Now get me a musician" (II Kings 3:15),—to coax prophecy to come to him. But it did not necessarily work. But Moshe [could receive prophecy] at any time that he wanted, as he said (Num.9:8), "Wait and I will hear what the Lord commands for you". Similarly, on the verse (Lev.16:2), "speak to your brother Aharon, that he should not come at any time to the Holy", the sages in Sifra said, "Aharon is [in the category of] 'he should not come [at any time],' but not Moshe.

Rambam Expounded On Moshe

You can see that Rambam spent a lot of effort describing Moshe. That must be because understanding Moshe is crucial to understanding our reality. For starters, Moshe is a primary example of the ideas expressed in previous chapters; people are born with particular talents that sometimes require strange or trying circumstances to coax those talents to the fore; the achievements they can muster are endless because Hashem has no limits. Hashem can endlessly provide new choices that lead to new heights. Read Moshe's story and you will see how Hashem did this for Moshe.

Moshe Operated On A Unique Level

The additional thought advanced by this chapter is that no human will ever understand Hashem as clearly as Moshe did. Moshe understood Hashem's reality in the clearest way possible for a human being. No one could surpass or equal him because it was a special gift granted by Hashem.

It would never be in Hashem's best interest to grant another prophet the same intense clarity granted to Moshe, for two reasons. First, the whole point of creating humanity was to coax individuals to create on their own, each in a unique way and at a unique level of competence. This would require a broad range of creative potential distributed over a variety of opportunities. Every range is defined by a low and high point. The high point of clarity about Hashem was occupied by Moshe.

Second, only Moshe was granted this high point for the sake of providing an incontestable source of clarity. If another prophet was granted the same clarity as Moshe, there would be a contest between the two. Unless the second one repeated Moshe's clarity exactly, in which case nothing would be gained anyway. The second person would not be unique. Just the opposite, he would be superfluous.

Moshe's Credentials

Hearing Hashem speak is an overwhelming experience. It is a communion with the creator of the universe! As Rambam surmises from written reports, an experience of prophecy made the prophet crumple into something like a catatonic trance or a deep slumber. Another description suggests that one's physical senses were unable to operate, as if short-circuited. This sounds right since physical senses would only get in the way of experiencing the totally non-physical Creator. Today, we might describe it as an out-of-world experience.

This is the way Exodus 20:15-16 describes it. When Hashem spoke the Ten Commandments from Sinai, all the people present experienced a divine revelation—prophecy. This experience so overwhelmed them that the people thought they were going to die. They ran to Moshe after hearing the first two commandments and pleaded with him to take over as the audience. They much preferred to hear the rest from Moshe instead of continuing to hear Hashem directly. Hashem agreed and spoke the last eight of the Ten Commandments to Moshe alone.

This publicly demonstrated that Moshe was the only one able to speak to Hashem without losing his senses. He had achieved such a high fluency with reality, clarity of Hashem, that he was able to speak to Hashem just as people speak to one another. How public was this demonstration? Numerous times the count is given in terms of men suitable for the military. It was just over 600,000. There must have been at least as many women, increasing the population to 1.2 million. Adding the children and seniors suggests a total population at Sinai of between 2-3 million people.

These numbers establish three vital elements of Moshe's credentials. First, a vast number of people—far more than with any other prophet—personally witnessed Moshe's communion with Hashem. Second, no one else in this vast crowd was able to commune the way Moshe did. Third, everyone agreed to the details of this record; there are no alternative narratives. (Later, we learn that Moshe could commune with Hashem whenever he wanted, another distinguishing feature that was not true for all other prophets, as Rambam expounded.)

How Was Moshe The Father Of All Prophets?
Moshe is called the father of all prophets, in the sense of head of the clan, because the whole nation testified to his superiority and no one before or since reached the level of his prophetic clarity—so, father of all prophets. It could have been different, as it is in most instances. For example, Galileo was considered the father of Physics until Sir Isaac Newton displaced him who, in turn, was displaced by Albert Einstein. Great men come and go and it is difficult for us lesser minds to rate such luminaries, especially not knowing their circumstances.

In this case, it was Hashem who rated Moshe at the top, not us.

Another reason Moshe is called the father of all prophets is that he "fathered" the certification process for future prophets, as per Hashem's instruction. Since the Sinai event will never be repeated, meaning there will never be another mass validation of a prophet, future prophets can only become validated in one of two ways. Either a previously known prophet vouches for a new prophet OR the applicant passes the test of prophecy.

Test A Prophet

The first test for prophecy is our own experience with the person. Do we know them as sufficiently wise, refined, and pious to qualify for a special communication from Hashem? If no, there is nothing to investigate and, if we persist, then we are just asking to be deceived.

If yes and they now claim to have such a communication, we ask them to prove it by predicting the future. It could be a simple prediction such as one inch of rain will fall tomorrow exactly between two and three in the afternoon. But, it has to be a precise prediction and it has to come true exactly as predicted. No discrepancies are allowed. Otherwise, it was not a revelation from Hashem, just an astute guess. Therefore, if more or less than one inch of rain falls at the exact time predicted, the person is considered a false prophet and deserving of a death penalty for trifling with divine matters.

If the prediction comes true, the person is validated as a prophet of Hashem, but only because he passed the test that Moshe established. We recognize he may have tricked us, somehow. It is only our confidence in Moshe's prophetic test for a true prophet that we accept him.

Thus, if a prophet would ever contradict Moshe's description of Hashem's Torah, we would immediately reject them by the following logic.

1. Moshe prophesied that a person who passes the test is a prophet.
2. Moshe prophesied that Hashem would never change the Torah conveyed to us by Moshe.
3. This #1 type prophet is contradicting #2 by saying Hashem is changing the Torah.
4. If we accept #3, then Moshe was wrong on #2.
5. But then Moshe may just as well have been wrong on #1.
6. Without confidence in #1, we have no reason to accept #3 which re-establishes #2.

Thus, it is a self-checking test with Moshe always being the final authority. Unless, of course, the supposed prophet in #3 performed miracles at least as great, and as widely witnessed, as Moshe's. That would work but Moshe's prophecy assured us that will never happen and it never has.

How Should We Test Ourselves?

The truth is that such a false prophet may honestly believe they are right. We have already seen great men who have failed in this way. Someone may very well experience something that convinces them that they now perceive reality better than Moshe did. Since they are honestly convinced, how can we hold them to a fault?

This question is more relevant than just for prophets. Every one of us is subject to such self-delusion! How can we protect ourselves against our own convictions? Eventually, they turn out to have been false, but we realize it too late.

The answer is the same as for other fields. Sometimes, people challenge the prevailing wisdom with a novel idea, but without proof. For example, a new virus appears and all the doctors advise one approach but one doctor insists on a different approach. The rebel doctor is not superior to his colleagues but argues his position with the greatest passion. (You may recognize this scenario from the stories that emerged during the Covid19 pandemic.)

We can only choose one approach and naturally we want the best possible outcome. "Do you have the credentials or the proof to outweigh your colleagues?" we ask. "If not," we continue, "you must be humble enough to realize that you might be missing something. Prove it or lose it."

We have to be humble enough to test ourselves the same way before championing any deviation from established Torah instructions.

Moshe's Most Important Lesson

Moshe started as a rebel of sorts who had to learn humility. Originally, he was an adopted prince in the royal household, destined for self-aggrandizement, but he finished as the humblest of all men, ever. Such progress was Moshe's own doing as I will demonstrate in the paragraph following the next. First, let it be acknowledged that this progress naturally led to his crowning achievement.

Moshe's humility allowed Hashem to communicate the divine Torah message through him without concern that Moshe would personalize it in any way. Moshe became the honest broker between Hashem and the people with whom Hashem wanted to communicate. Humility was the key to functioning as an honest broker.

The Torah hints of the steps Moshe took to become the classic example of humility. Before Moshe was selected to lead the Jewish people, we are told three stories of how he acted on his own (Ex.2:11-3:1). The first occurred while he was living in Pharaoh's palace. Moshe went out to see the burdens of his fellow Jews and wound up killing an Egyptian to save the life of a fellow Jew. The second recounted how he, a stranger, protected the shepherd daughters of Yisro (Jethro, in English) from their bullying male counterparts at the water spring in far-off Midian. (This led to his marriage to one of Yisro's daughters.) The third seems to be a throwaway line. As a preface to his famous encounter at the burning bush, it mentions that Moshe shepherded Yisro's flock deep into the wilderness.

I suggest that each of these stories hint at a new phase in Moshe's humbling himself to the reality around him. The first story unfolded because he felt for his fellow Jews even though he personally was well taken care of. Moshe humbled himself in favor of his kinsmen. That is not so unusual, but it is a good start.

The second story showed he had graduated from caring for his own and was now willing to take up the plight of strangers. That is rare but not unheard of.

The third story informs us that Moshe did not want to pasture the sheep on land that might belong to someone else, so he took the flock "deep into the wilderness". This phrase informs us that his concern had broadened past family and past strangers to include unseen landowners who might not care. They might not even exist! Call this a standout performance.

Having self-developed thus far, Hashem motivates Moshe to continue on that path. First impressions are important and the very first thing Hashem says to Moshe at the burning bush is, "remove your shoes". "What kind of man has no shoes", I have asked many people. The usual answer is "a poor person". Once we tune in to the correct channel, it is clear that Hashem's first message to Moshe was "impoverish yourself, humble yourself". At the end of the story, Hashem attests to how well Moshe took this first message to heart by naming him, "the humblest of all men" (Num.12:3).

Moshe's secret to seeing the reality of Hashem was his ability to self-negate, to pierce through the illusions common to this world such as position, power, authority, etc. and see instead the reality laid out by Hashem.

The importance of self-negation coincides with the "universe" idea I expressed earlier wherein I described the nothingness from which the universe emerged. I used a simplified example: It is as if the Creator took a piece of nothing (0), divided it in two (0=+1-1), and called one half "positive" and the other half "negative".

We call each half "energy", either positive or negative. Energy would then become matter as in the equation $E=mc^2$ and the universe takes on form—or seems to. It is all really nothing. Moshe realized that, relative to Hashem, it is all really nothing.

All Or Nothing

Self-negation also happens to us. It always happens to some degree, over time. Hashem designed us that way. Babies are born with undeveloped intelligence. All they know is the hunger that pains them and the strangeness that frightens them. Through no fault of their own, they are self-centered from day one.

As a baby grows from infancy to full size, the range of experience grows, but always with a self-centered mooring. This is my bed, this is my house, this is my street, this is my school—everything in terms of "me" because that is the original yardstick against which everything is measured. Thus, our early years build up a habit of self-importance.

Habits are hard to kick, but kick them we do, slowly, over time. Slowly, we discover other "me's" who favor their own self-importance over ours. We start to negotiate with others, other "me's", for what "me" needs or wants. The natural process is to learn that "me" is not the only one; then to learn that "me" is not the center; then to learn that "me" actually enjoys others; ultimately to learn that "me" would sacrifice everything for this new baby we just made—"me" needs nothing.

That is the universal program that Hashem built into the system so that each person would at least dabble with self-negation. The goal is for each individual to create their own such program because, paradoxically, the more one negates oneself, the more real one becomes. It is a universal idea.

Answer to: Why Moshe Our Teacher, Not Our Prophet? Before abolishing prophecy, Hashem made sure humanity had experienced several prophet types, including the best. Each tried to connect us to the reality of our Creator. The very clearest connection to Hashem was expressed by Moshe, the humblest of all men.

That is why we never call him Moshe, our savior, even though he delivered us from slavery, or Moshe, our lawgiver, even though he conveyed to us the Ten Commandments, or Moshe, our prophet, even though he foretold our destiny, but always Moshe, our teacher, because like every iconic teacher, he inspired us to be like him.

8 - Who Wrote The Book?

<u>The Familiar Ani Ma'amin</u>: I believe with complete faith that the entire Torah now in our hands is the same one that was given to Moshe, our teacher, peace be upon him.

My Critique: This Ani ma'amin emphasizes the accuracy of the documents we have preserved over the generations. The next Ani ma'amin proclaims the everlasting quality of the original Torah. This reverses the order of Rambam's 8th and 9th statements, an order I find more logical. As can be seen below, Rambam here emphasized the divine quality of what Moshe originally wrote, an orderly step in his argument. Only after that is established will it be worthwhile to claim that we have a faithful copy of the original divine words.

<u>The Yigdal Couplet</u>:
God gave His people a Torah of truth,
by means of His prophet, the most trusted of His household;

My Critique: This together with the next couplet captures Rambam's point about the quality of Moshe's Torah.

Rambam's eighth description of reality: The Torah is from Heaven. This Torah given to us through Moshe, our teacher, is completely from the mouth of the Almighty. It all came to Moshe from Hashem in a manner that is metaphorically called speech. No one knows the exact experience except Moshe himself—since it was unique to him. Moshe was like a scribe who is dictated to and writes down all of the events, the stories, and the commandments. Therefore, Moshe is called the engraver.

There is no difference between "the sons of Cham were Kush and Mitzrayim" (Gen.10:6), "his wife's name was Mehitabel" (Gen.36:39), "Timnah was his concubine" (Gen.36:12), on the one hand, and "I am the Lord, your Hashem" (Ex.20:2) and "Hear Israel" (Deut.6:4), on the other. They are all from the mouth of the Almighty and it is all Torah of Hashem—complete, pure, and holy truth.

Anyone who says, "These types of verses or stories were written by Moshe on his own," is deemed by our sages and prophets a worse and more brazen heretic than all others. That is because he considers the Torah to have both original and extraneous parts; meaning that the chronicles and stories don't contain a Divine message but were inserted by Moshe. The sages (Sanhedrin 99a) considered this heresy (denying the Torah came from Heaven) to include even one who accepts the divine origin of the whole Torah except for one verse, any verse, claiming Moshe inserted it, not the Holy One. Such people are covered by the verse "Since he disgraced the word of the Lord" (Num.13:31).

Rather, every single word of the Torah contains wisdom and wonders for the one who analyzes them. Torah's ultimate wisdom is never fully grasped, as its measure is longer than the earth and broader than the sea. One should always walk in the footsteps of David, who prayed, "Uncover my eyes and I shall look upon the wonders of Your Torah" (Ps.119:18).

In addition, the traditional understanding of the Torah is also from the Almighty. Thus, the particular formats in which we continue to make the *sukkah*, the *lulav*, the *shofar*, the *tsitsit*, the *tefilllin* and other such matters, is the exact form that Hashem said to Moshe, as Moshe reliably told to us. The statement asserting this principle is, "with this shall you know that it is the Lord that sent me to do all of these acts, and it is not from my heart" (Num.16:28).

In the previous chapter, **Rambam** established how Moshe was able to raise his vision by lowering his eyes. Through self-negation, Moshe understood Hashem's reality in the clearest way possible for a human being.

No one would ever surpass or equal him because it was a special gift granted by Hashem. Good for him! What about us?

Clarity Is Hard To Teach

How does one transmit clarity? How does one describe to another a vision or experience they had that the other did not? It requires an abundance of words and some simulations.

We know this difficulty from trying to teach our children. "Do not step off the sidewalk," a parent might warn a young child, "so you don't get hit by a car." If they disobey, the parent might spank the child's backside and respond to their outcry with, "a car would hurt even more because it goes faster and sharper than my hand." That lesson is much easier to deliver than longer-term concerns such as "brush your teeth so you don't get cavities" or "study for your exams so you will get a good job" or "don't snack too much so you don't get fat." It is much harder to picture or simulate long-term concerns, especially when there are many to teach about. It takes a lot of time and a lot of examples.

Over the course of time, Hashem had provided many prophets to guide humanity. We know that Hashem spoke to Adam, Noach, Shem, Avraham, Yitzchak, Yaakov, Aaron, and Bilaam. We know this from Moshe's written testimony, not from anything they wrote. Hashem hadn't asked any of these previous prophets to publish because, in the early generations, the creativity that Hashem wanted from humanity had to be much more open-ended. Had one prophet carved his vision in stone, so to speak, it might have been very difficult for another to create a new relationship with Hashem. As it was, mistakes were made and official documentation would have perpetuated such mistakes. Indeed, it was probably the lack of documentation that allowed Moshe to question past performance, identify errors, and develop his better clarity.

Best To Write It Down
Even though Moshe had forty years in the wilderness to teach his lessons, the people would never attain his clarity and their descendants would certainly not. Especially since Moshe's clarity about Hashem consisted of an immense database that constitutes reality. Consequently, Hashem finally said, "write this song down for yourselves" (Deut.31:19). This instruction refers not only to the song that follows shortly in the text but also to all the five books that Moshe wrote.

Moshe's words are called a song because they are like the words of a song or poem that uses stylistic tricks to convey much more than the surface meaning. It is as if Hashem said, "Your words will be the condensed version of all the humanly possible exactness about

Hashem that you have experienced and taught; they will be an anchor to that truth for all future generations."

Since Moshe had the clearest vision possible, he became the first prophet whom Hashem told to publish his prophecy. His words could serve as the proof text for all future prophetic writings—do they concur with the best vision which is the original we already have?

Moshe's clarity resulted in his writings being considered words dictated by Hashem. We don't know whether Hashem created letters in the air for Moshe to see or a voice for Moshe to hear or a mental conviction that Moshe could only convey in certain words. In any case, the communication was from Hashem and the words themselves were divine.

Not so for the other prophets. After Moshe, other prophets were instructed by Hashem to publish their visions and the resulting books complete the twenty-four books of the Torah. The visions of other prophets were clear to them—otherwise, Hashem would not have entrusted them to deliver a message—but the words they wrote to describe their visions were their own words, not Hashem's. The visions other prophets saw were filtered through a lens of their personality—they never reached Moshe's level of self-negation. That is why none of their books have the same authority or sanctity as Moshe's five books. None of them.

The Superior Quality of Moshe's Words

It is amazing to realize that no other prophet, Jewish or otherwise, ever claimed to record the exact words Hashem spoke as Moshe did. The true prophets never claimed it because it wasn't true. Of course! But why didn't the false prophets make such a claim? Since they were apparently able to promote a lie about themselves, why didn't they give themselves the maximum authority, equal to the bar Moshe had already set? The answer must be that Hashem never allowed such aspirations to enter their heads.

The superior quality of Moshe's words must be burned into our minds. They are not more true than the words of the other prophets because all real prophets spoke the truth. Rather, Moshe's words are more pregnant with the truth. They broadcast truth through every facet of their letters, their pronunciation, their meaning, their order, and their selection or omission.

Moshe Also Explained The Text

Text can always be read in different ways and with different emphases. Ancient texts are especially vulnerable to this ambiguity since it comes with no punctuation at all. Hashem overcame this obvious fault line by having Moshe orally explain the text on many levels, like a poem, over the forty years of wilderness. (The lack of punctuation thus became an improvement to the text because it allowed the text to be parsed in more than one way.)

In Chapter 1, I demonstrated how the opening letters of Moshe's first book, *Breishis*, expound on the physics of creation.

Talmud literature is full of behavioral messages derived from hints in the Torah text. For example, an unusual spelling of *YaDCHa* teaches to wear tefillin on our left (weaker) hand. Also, the three exact repetitions against cooking a young lamb in its mother's milk lay down three levels of prohibition. This also led to our cautious custom of waiting as much as six hours after eating meat before eating any dairy products to always keep the two food types separate.

We have an ancient teaching that Hashem composed the Torah before creating the universe and later revealed this composition to Moshe. What this means is the Torah describes the concepts that drove the construction of the universe. For example, since the Torah requires fringes on a four-cornered garment, therefore, Hashem included on our planet the need for clothes, the ability to weave clothes from fibers, the simple geometry of a four-cornered object, and so on. In other words, Hashem used the Torah as a blueprint to construct the universe.

Today we might explain that, just as numeric equations can describe the universe mathematically and geometric coordinates can plot the world in digitized form, so too the words of the Torah constitute a code that describes the universe. After all, words and letters are symbols the same way digital code is. What description of the universe do the words of the Torah provide? All types, including physics, chemistry, and geometry—you just have to decipher the words in the appropriate way. However, the most important message of the Torah words, the one on the surface, describes the universe in terms of best behavior practices.

Do not consider this reference to codes a cute, new subterfuge to satisfy modern sophistication. Already thousands of years ago, Jewish sages were referencing codes within the text of the Torah. One code relies on using the numerical value of the letters. Samples of this were discussed in Chapter 1.

Another code relies on forming a new word by substituting some or all its letters for a coded counterpart. One famous example of this is called *AT-BaSH* because it replaces the first letter in the alphabet, *A(lef)* with the last letter, *T(of)* and the second letter, *B(ais)* with the second-last letter *SH(in)* and so on, and then interpreting the result. The underlying premise of this code is that a mirror image can shed light on the original.

The Bible Code

Other ancient sages found hidden messages in Moshe's books by reading every 5th letter or every 7th letter or the like. Skipping a set number of letters and reading the results lends itself easily to computer searching, even when the number of letters skipped is very large. The results of such computer searches came to be known as the bible code method. Skipping large blocks of letters uncovered quite a few clusters of historical events which suggested the Torah predicted these events by clustering them together. Some claimed this was proof of the Torah's divine origin. Others claimed they could skip letters to find similar "predictions" in any large text, such as *War and Peace*.

The nub of the argument hinged on how objectively each side had selected the "predictions" before the search began. Some diehards still fight this battle but the "divine origin" side disbanded early to avoid charlatan claims with which they did not want to be associated. One famous charlatan claim came from Michael Drosnin who wrote a bestseller called *The Bible Code* (Touchstone, 1997) predicated on using this method to predict the future. Of course, he couldn't prove it but the claim was bold enough to earn him fame and fortune.

I taught the bible codes for a while before the controversy hit and, to this day, remain convinced they are real. However, not the way Drosnin pretended and maybe not even the way the "divine origin" side claimed. I remain convinced about the bible codes because the divine origin of the Torah can be determined from other angles, some of which I presented above. Since the Torah was written by Hashem, it makes sense that Torah is true from every angle, whether that be by skipping letters, transposing letters, reading the numerical equivalents, or a host of other possible codes.

However, Torah will also contain codes describing all possible future events, of which, most will never happen. This contention is based on the way I reconciled our free choice with Hashem's knowledge of the future in Chapter 4 above. Consequently, no one can use the bible codes to predict the future we finally choose because other futures are equally possible and are also predicted in the Torah; they just do not show unless one uses a different code such as AT-Ba<u>SH</u>, for example. Who can know which code to use? Perhaps, not even Hashem because Hashem is waiting to see our free choice.

Reality For Women
Moshe's clarity was for all people's benefit but not all the mitzvahs he taught applied to all people. The well-known reality is that different people need different instructions.

To provide a simple example, most of us do not need medical training to the depth that doctors do. In that vein, more than half of the Torah's 613 instructions only addressed the kohens who worked in the Temple. Non-kohens never performed these instructions and today, with no Temple, not even kohens are able to perform them.

About thirty of the remaining mitzvah instructions were never incumbent on women. In some circles, this has led to quite a controversy. They complain this is discriminatory. They forget or ignore the fact that Hashem always discriminates by parceling out unique potentials and challenges for each individual. Still, the Torah suggests patience in the face of such complaints. After all, everybody is jealous of someone else's privileges at some point or another. (Do not take this last comment as license or permission to be jealous. Do not even take it as a reason to be jealous.)

My suspicion is that women do not need the thirty or so extra instructions to guide their spiritual development (which is what the mitzvah instructions are all about)—they have more natural inclinations in this area. The extra mitzvah instructions would only misguide them. In fact, you might say that the extra instructions might stifle the broader creativity of which women are capable and are tasked with discovering such as through the relationships they nurture.

Reality For Non-Jews

Non-Jews were given seven broad categories of instructions within which we find many of the details later instructed to the Jewish people. Hashem gave these instructions to Adam, Noah and other early leaders but none seem to have recorded these ancient instructions. We only know of them from Moshe's testimony in his Torah.

Moshe instructed non-Jews because, after all, they too are subject to reality. Indeed, the Pesach story relates that a great number of non-Jews accompanied the Jewish people out of Egypt. It is not clear what happened to them. Perhaps, they converted and became part of the Jewish people, perhaps they drifted away, or perhaps they retained a non-Jewish identity within the Jewish nation. An example of this last possibility is exhibited today by the many non-Jews who are citizens of the modern State of Israel, some reaching a very high position in society. Whatever the case, reality cannot be ignored, not then and not now. Moshe's instructions provided clarity about reality not only for those who joined him but also for all peoples of all times.

The nations at the time knew of Moshe's miracles. How could they not, considering he caused the downfall of the superpower of the time? They could have joined the transformation but chose not to. Most non-Jewish peoples preferred to stick to the culture with which they were familiar. As always, Hashem would not force them to recognize reality. On the other hand, allowing the entire world to persist in the evil practices that emerge from ignorance of reality would thwart Hashem's purpose in creation. Such worldwide ignorance might even overflow onto the Jews and rob them of the clarity they had attained. Remedial action was necessary.

Christianity and Islam

Rambam (Laws of Kings 11:4) maintains that Hashem inspired the onset of Christianity and Islam (and probably others too far away for Rambam to know about) so that non-Jews would have their own version to which they would subscribe because it was their own. Even though their version could not and would not be as clear as Moshe's, at least, it would coax them to acknowledge the reality of one creator. This could eventually lead them to all the other truths that follow, especially when prodded by the truth persistently exemplified by the Jewish people.

I am not suggesting that Hashem purposely misled the architects of Christianity and Islam into something less than the truth. Rather, I think the truth so impassioned them that they became fervent about proselytizing it to others. To bring more and more followers into the fold, they diluted the message to make it more palatable.

The Temptation To Dilute

I can attest to this temptation from personal experience. When I first went out into the world to teach Torah, it was to a far-off community that was not very religious. Before going, I respectfully took my leave from my mentor R. Yaakov Weinberg, ob"m, at which time he warned me to make sure I was teaching the proper details. I nodded to assure him that I would but his request actually bothered me in the back of my mind. R. Weinberg was the one who granted me the title Rabbi—he must have believed I knew my stuff. Was he now backtracking on that?

It didn't take long for me to find out what he meant. As I began teaching Torah life to people who were reluctant to actually practice it, I found myself looking for ways to water down the requirements so as to make them more palatable. I wanted to "make the sale" and easier rules seemed more salable. It was only the memory of my mentor's warning that pushed me to find more resonant explanations for the religious truths I taught rather than water them down for easier swallowing.

I try to find "more resonance" by piggybacking a new truth onto an old, established one. A particular event sticks in my mind. I had been discussing school business with a prominent member of the Board who, himself, was not religious but whose children were. On the Board, this member was one of the strongest defenders of our education strategy. He was proud that his children had become religious through our school, probably because their behavior had become more refined and their studies more serious. Knowing about this pride of his, I figured his non-attendance at services was just due to old, die-hard habits. Imagine my shock when this Board member offhandedly mentioned that he didn't believe in God. Why was he pleased his children were religious?

However, since he was an intelligent man not prone to inner contradictions, I confronted him. "Sam," I said, "do you believe in being honest?" "Of course!" he replied. "How about helping others?" I continued. "Sure, as a lawyer, I regularly do some pro bono work," he assured me. "Are you optimistic about the future?" I probed. "Yes, I guess I am," he surmised. "Well," I continued, "you must believe in God because otherwise, you have no reason to act that way. There is no reason to suffer for being honest when only you know the truth, no reason to be charitable to someone who will never be able to help you back, and especially no reason to be hopeful in a dog-eat-dog world. You just don't like to call it God because it is not fashionable." I would have liked Sam to say "I never thought of it that way" but instead he said, "You're good." Maybe that is why I remember the exchange.

Monotheistic concepts are ennobling in themselves and eventually win the day but, as we all know, reality can be hard to confront. We may have trouble recognizing our own inner contradictions, but we can often detect it in others. Frequently, we detect it when politicians fail to deliver on their campaign promises for fear of offending part of the electorate. Non-Jewish prophets also faced an electorate, of sorts. The truths Hashem revealed to non-Jewish prophets would be a hard sell to their audience. A tempting approach is to water them down for easier consumption. But, over the distance of time, these dilutions have led to a totally different target.

It has been the particular mandate of the Jewish people through the centuries to accurately preserve and exemplify the teachings of Moshe for the benefit of all. It is the mandate of all non-Jewish peoples to create the humility that accepts that accuracy and the benefit the teachings of Moshe convey.

Answer to: Who Wrote The Book? Hashem graced Moshe with divine words that encode within them the reality of Hashem's creation. Those words became the Five Books of Moshe, known collectively as the Torah. Subsequent books by later prophets were also called Torah as a shorthand way of affirming their truth and holiness but were never accorded the same status as Moshe's.

Moshe also taught us how to interpret the words he wrote. The combination of the written and oral words captures the clarity of Hashem's reality that Moshe saw and experienced.

Moshe's words do not focus on picturing Hashem who remains without body and invisible. Such a focus would probably overwhelm us, as did the Sinai experience. Or such focus would remain incomprehensible, which amounts to the same thing.

Instead, Moshe's words describe our reality in terms of behavior. This coincides with what we know about actions; the ones we take or avoid affect the way we think. Our behaviors should be considered as coded keystrokes that guide and support our minds to create relationships the way Hashem creates.

The next chapter will describe how the Jewish people have gone to extraordinary lengths to preserve Moshe's clarity through the generations of Jewish and human development.

9 - Times Change, What Now?

<u>The Familiar Ani Ma'amin</u>: I believe with complete faith that this Torah will not be exchanged nor will there be another Torah from the Creator, blessed is His Name.

My Critique: As pointed out in the previous chapter, this and the previous Ani Ma'amin reverse the order of Rambam's 8th and 9th statements. As can be seen below, Rambam here emphasized the reliability of the transmission of the Torah, not its Divine origin. It baffles me why the Ani ma'amin author switched the order of Rambam's 8th and 9th points.

<u>The Yigdal Couplet</u>:
God will never amend nor exchange His law
for any other one, for all eternity.

My Critique: This together with the previous couplet captures Rambam's point about the quality of Moshe's Torah.

> **Rambam's ninth description of reality:** This Torah has faithfully been transmitted from the Creator, Hashem, and not from anyone else. It cannot be added to and it cannot be taken away from, as it is

stated, "you shall not add to it and you shall not take away from it" (Deut.13:1). We have already elucidated this principle in the introduction to this composition.

Rambam: After Moshe, we will never have a clearer insight into the reality Hashem has created for us. Any change to the Torah, which is the only written version of Moshe's clarity, would blur that reality and that is why the Torah text can never change, neither on purpose nor by accident.

On Purpose

Times change, don't we have to change with them? No, and yes. No, times do not really change, not as far as humans go. As the saying goes, we still have to put on our pants one leg at a time. Our physical, emotional, and spiritual needs do not change even though we might have difficulty prioritizing them. Hashem provided Torah instructions to help with that. Following them gives us the confidence of ultimate fulfillment.

Yes, times do change because, as per our mandate, we humans create new realities about which we have not yet developed any clarity. We become confused. That is why Hashem also provided sages of extraordinary intelligence and piety in every generation to guide us.

Every generation should follow the advice of those sages who honor Torah instructions.

When doing so, we dare not confuse their intelligence with Hashem's. If we did, that would contaminate the divine purity of the original instructions which would ultimately undermine our confidence in them. Therefore, whatever instructions the sages add to our repertoire must be kept separate from the text of the Torah. They are good words but not Hashem's words. (I give examples below.)

Another reason to maintain the integrity of the divine text is to preserve the codes embedded in them. Even though most of the information embedded is hidden, it must remain available for discovery by a future sage or a computer program, as outlined in the previous chapter.

By Accident
Despite our best efforts, a comparison of ancient scrolls from different parts of the globe has revealed about six discrepancies from one to the other. Only single letters differ and they are all silent so that one person listening to another reading a different scroll would not detect a mismatch to his text.

Although we have exercised as much due diligence as possible, there is no guarantee that the text version we have chosen as our standard matches the original exactly. If it does match the original, that will no doubt be thanks to Hashem's hidden help. If it doesn't, then we have a slightly wrong version. Still, even if we made all the wrong choices between the versions, we do not have to worry that the message has been corrupted because the particular letters in question do not affect the surface message.

Preserving The Words of Moshe
Given that Moshe's publication was to be the ultimate repository of Hashem's reality, there had to be methods of preserving the text accurately, even down to the level of the individual letters. Without photocopiers, safeguards were needed to ensure that human error did not creep into the copies. Miracles could have been deployed for that but Hashem prefers humans to use their own effort, care, and concern to create safeguards.

Hashem exemplified this by providing the first safeguard. Every male was instructed to write his own copy of the five books, even if he inherited one from his father. This ensured everyone learned to read and write and become familiar with the text, highly unusual in ancient times. It also ensured sufficient copies from which to study, which was the next safeguard. If you ever heard that the Jewish people are known as the people of the book, this is why.

As an even stronger safeguard, Hashem instructed that every male diligently study and know the contents of the five books. Widespread knowledge of the text would forestall errors from creeping into the text. Since there was little else to do during the forty wilderness years, Torah study quickly became the national pastime. After the wilderness years, they began to conquer the land. But they didn't have to forsake their studies in favor of developing military might because miracles were provided to ease the conquest. When you know your fate depends on miracles, you persist in your spiritual quest. That is what they did.

Our Turn To Help

As a further safeguard, and as another challenge to our creativity, Hashem instructed the Judiciary to construct social standards that would encourage Torah knowledge. Moshe was the first head of the court so it fell to him to set the pace in this regard. One of his innovations legislated that a different portion of the Torah be read publicly every Shabbat morning. When you might be called to read for the public, you make sure you know how and what to read.

The fact that Moshe introduced the instruction as his own and did not paint it as an instruction from Hashem, which he could have easily done, is a good example of what I wrote above. Admitting that the legislation was his own idea emphasized the need to always differentiate between Hashem's instructions and man-made instructions, however highly inspired. This requirement to remember even the history of an instruction fostered our attention down to the smallest details of the instructions.

The public reading of the Torah was not just an exercise in public education; it was also a test for the accuracy of the scroll being read. To this day, public readings must be always done from a handwritten scroll which keeps alive the need to be ever-vigilant about the accuracy of the text. It often happens that a reader will stop his public reading when he notices a possible error in the handwritten scroll from which he is reading. Or, a listener will stop a public reader with the complaint that the reading did not match his text. The discrepancy will have to be resolved before continuing. The scroll must be 100% accurate, otherwise, it is set aside until corrected. If that is no longer practicable, the scroll is buried to assure its error does not migrate to other copies. This is true for even small errors such as an extra letter, a missing letter, or even two letters touching each other.

Instructions formulated by Moshe or other sages are not immutable the way Hashem's instructions are. Accordingly, a thousand years later, Ezra extended Moshe's idea of public reading by adding three more time slots, namely, Monday and Thursday mornings and

Shabbat afternoons. These readings guarantee that three days do not elapse without a public reading of the Torah.

The natural result of such instructions was that studying remained a national pastime and scholarship the highest calling. Hashem's promise that Moshe's instructions will never be forgotten through all the generations of the Jewish people would never require a blatant display of Divine intervention, something that Hashem always avoids. Instead, a chance encounter between a gifted teacher and an extra studious soul would be the only arrangement Hashem needed to keep the promise.

Moshe Also Explained The Text

The preservation of that oral teaching was assigned the same importance as preserving the written word. The study of the written and oral Torah together is what occupied the attention of Moshe and the people of Israel during the entire forty years in the wilderness. Even afterward, young men were always charged with mastering this material before they assumed the rest of their adult responsibilities. This is the way all complicated fields of study are mastered and transmitted, with a text and an oral explanation from a renowned expert.

Nevertheless, over the centuries, and especially after the destruction of the First Temple and the subsequent exile, scholarship declined. There arose many different questions about minor issues that had not previously been relevant. For example, everyone, without exception, meticulously observed Shabbat. This included not lighting a fire on Shabbat. Since it never happened, the sages disputed what consequence would follow if someone ever did light a fire. No one could point to a historical consequence because it had never happened. These differences were debated more for their theoretical value than anything else. Eventually, these debates were recorded in writing because they became too numerous and sophisticated to rely on memory alone. The record of these debates and their conclusions is the Talmud.

Such errors and memory losses were foreseen by Hashem, of course, and a protocol was assigned for their resolution. Mostly, the protocol was to follow the majority opinion but not everybody's opinion was counted. It was well understood that many would be tempted to find the path of least resistance. Therefore, the only ones counted were those who qualified in two ways; they followed the instructions of the Torah with scrupulous piety and they displayed expert mastery of the entire range of Torah scholarship. Scrupulous piety alone tends to crown itself with unnecessary strictures while master scholarship alone invites clever over permissiveness. As long as both qualifications were present, no open miracles were necessary for Hashem to guarantee (see Is. 59:21) that the original message would always be preserved.

Did We Add New Torah?

Given these rules of transmission, I must now explain why new books were added to the Torah. Conceivably, allowing additions to the Torah could detract from its hitherto unchallenged authority. Nevertheless, they were formulated to record the successes and failures of the Jewish people's attempt to create a new country, culture, and society based on Moshe's teachings. We can learn much from our past. As an extreme example, the Megillas Esther introduces the holiday of Purim which showcases the sweeping powers of the Judiciary to introduce new instructions provided they are properly identified as Rabbinic in origin rather than Divine.

Answer to: Times Change, What Now? Time hasn't changed for Hashem. To reach the goal of creating people who could themselves create, Hashem had to provide a wide range of talents that people could develop and make their own. Hashem also had to provide a wide range of histories and circumstances in which they could do so.

Prophecy was a very necessary talent to guide people through the invisible labyrinth of ideas, histories, and relationships. Prophets needed to prove they were prophets because the value of their guidance was not testable. Moshe's credentials as a prophet were unassailable so his prophecy could act as the benchmark for other prophecies.

Hashem perpetuated Moshe's clarity of reality by giving him the words to describe its essence. Hashem's reality being constant, the words will never need changing and Hashem arranges that they never suffer a significant loss of accuracy.

The Jewish people's extraordinary efforts in every generation to preserve the accuracy of the text are recognized by even non-Jews. For example, Bible.org states, "As a result of this extreme care, the quality of the manuscripts of the Hebrew Bible surpasses all other ancient manuscripts."

10 - Why Do The Innocent Suffer?

<u>The Familiar Ani Ma'amin</u>: I believe with complete faith that the Creator, blessed is His Name, knows all the deeds of human beings and their thoughts, as it is said, 'He fashions their hearts all together, He comprehends all their deeds.'

My Critique: This author adds "and their thoughts" to Rambam's words. At first, I thought he was just filling in what Rambam meant to say. Then I realized that he doesn't quote any of the verses cited by Rambam but instead adds his own. True, the verse he quotes does support his statement about both deeds and thoughts but it also shows me that he meant to quarrel with Rambam, not condense him. Shocking!

<u>The Yigdal Couplet</u>:

He scrutinizes and knows our hiddenmost secrets;–
He perceives a matter's outcome at its inception.

My Critique: This too might be a misrepresentation if "hiddenmost secrets" refer to people's thoughts. However, it could refer to "hidden actions", things we do that we don't want others to know about. The reference to perceiving an outcome might prove that interpretation.

> **Rambam's tenth description of reality:** Hashem knows the actions of people and does not ignore them. Not like the opinion of the one who said, 'the Lord abandoned the earth,' but rather as it is stated, "Great of counsel and mighty of works, as Your eyes are open upon all the ways of people, etc." (Jer.32:19); "And the Lord saw that the evil of man was mighty upon the earth, etc." (Gen.6:5); and it is stated (Gen.18:2), "the yelling of Sodom and Ammorah, as it was mighty."

I contend that this principle of **Rambam** will uncover for us how merciful Hashem can allow so many widespread calamities to befall innocent victims. It defies belief that every victim in a crowd deserved the same fate. But, if they didn't and Hashem couldn't save them, what is the use in worshiping Hashem? Before I answer this question, I must first admit that I diverge from the way most others understand this principle.

The Common Understanding
Most authorities use this principle to describe Hashem's omniscience. My fellow student of many years ago, Rabbi Mordechai Blumenfeld, claims our teacher and master, Rabbi Yaakov Weinberg, explained this principle

in conjunction with the next one, as follows. With regard to all our thoughts, speech, and actions, the tenth one says Hashem knows them and the eleventh one says Hashem reacts to them (*Fundamentals and Faith*, Targum Press, 1991 and repeated by Aish.com).

On the surface, these presentations make sense because omniscience is the necessary prerequisite for the appropriate reaction of reward or punishment. However, I find this interpretation of Rambam's tenth principle untenable for three reasons.

First, every religion has to define three components; the nature of Hashem, what communication Hashem has made to us, and what consequences would result from conforming or not conforming to said communication. Without defining these three components, no religion could exist. Rambam expanded these three categorical requirements into thirteen details to further clarify them, not to muddy them. Omniscience belongs in the first group that describes Hashem, not here in the last group. It is completely unlike Rambam to commit such an error of organization.

Second, omniscience has already been covered. In Chapter 2, I explored how Hashem created us with nothing more than a mindset which means Hashem's mind maintains us and so must always be aware of everything we think and do. In Chapter 4, I even posited that Hashem knows all future possibilities and chooses reactions to our behavior that will guarantee the result Hashem wants—another proof that Hashem's omniscience has already been covered.

Third, this tenth principle marks the beginning of Rambam's explanation of the third component, the consequences. We should be looking here for some new insight about consequences, not about omniscience.

My Understanding
I submit that Rambam's intent in this principle can best be uncovered by searching for answers to the following questions.

Why does Rambam only mention "actions" and not also "thoughts"? He certainly agrees that Hashem knows all thoughts as well as actions.

Why does Hashem's knowledge of people's actions guarantee "not ignoring them" or "not abandoning the earth"? The connection is vague.

Why did Rambam select these three verses to prove his point? The first references the pending exile that Yeremiahu had been warning about for some time, the second talks about the rampant corruption in the time of Noah, and the third talks about the viciously evil society of Sodom and Gomorrah. Each verse talks about a widely visible failure that didn't need omniscience to discover.

My answer to these questions began to take shape from focusing on why Rambam here only mentions actions but not thoughts. Thoughts are what I have been writing about. Hashem's overall goal is for each human to create like Hashem creates, with his or her mind. Realize that when the Torah says Hashem spoke and there was light, etc., the "speaking" is the Torah's way of describing the concretization of Hashem's thoughts. It couldn't be actual speaking because that would require a mouth and vocal cords but Hashem has no body.

Thoughts. On this score, every mental creation of ours is valid, even negative ones that lead to errors—we must first conceive them in order to refine them or reject them.

However, once private ideas and relationships are expressed physically, they start to affect others and are no longer private the way they were when they were just thoughts. The more physical the expression, the greater the effect. For example, if I have a negative thought, I will feel bad (resentful, jealous, victimized, etc.) but it will only be me because nobody else will be aware of my thought.

Once I share the thought by speaking it, that gives it a modest physical expression and some listeners may feel as negative as I do. But probably not for long. Disturbing sounds can be drowned out (ie. overwritten) by more comforting sounds and/or experiences.

However, once I act out my thought, it becomes vivid and more prone to response; some might join me and some might oppose me but, either way, people become significantly affected. Sometimes, that can snowball and cause people to act in ways they never would have otherwise.

When Must Hashem Intervene?

The preceding recounts how actions produce repercussions. Not every new idea leads to a positive outcome. What if Hashem did not want these repercussions to occur because they would steer humanity too sharply on the wrong course? Then Hashem will have to step in to forestall such results.

Earlier, in Chapter 4, I described how Hashem uses the knowledge of all future possibilities—I called them moves, as in a checkers game—to counter the choices that people make so that Hashem's goals are met—so that Hashem "wins the game". Constant management is required, as opposed to absent-minded abandonment. I contend that this is what Rambam says quite openly in this principle.

Hashem's knowledge of people's actions means Hashem knows where such actions will lead; Hashem cannot ignore the wrongheaded direction society sometimes takes. As Rambam put it, Hashem's reaction is "not ignoring them" and "not abandoning the earth". To reset the direction, Hashem will introduce a game-changer.

The verses Rambam quoted exemplify this message. At the time of Yeremiahu, Hashem determined that the Jewish people had lost their way and could be salvaged only with the most brutal of traumas. The trauma would be the destruction of the Temple and the exile of the people, as Yeremiahu prophesied. But hope in the future would eventually heal that trauma. Accordingly, Yeremiahu is told to purchase a field and safeguard the deed to publicize that the very person warning of impending exile was nevertheless confident of return and recovery. The verse quoted is the beginning of Yeremiahu's praise when he realizes how carefully Hashem manages history. "Great of counsel and mighty of works, as Your eyes are open upon all the ways of people, etc." (Jer.32:19).

The second verse quoted is about the flood in Noah's time. Society became so depraved that it needed a restart through the survival of one family. Ultimately, Hashem promised never to let it go that bad again, meaning that Hashem would have to step in sooner. "And the Lord saw that the evil of man was mighty upon the earth, etc." (Gen.6:5).

The third verse quoted is from the destruction of Sodom and Ammorah. One man, Abraham, was reintroducing the idea of one Hashem. His modus operandi was kindness, as if to say since we all stem from the same source, we ought to look after each other. The society of Sodom and Ammorah stood for the opposite. They treated the richness of their land as proprietary, not to be shared with others. Hashem determined that their example so threatened to drown out Abraham's message that it needed to be expunged; "the yelling of Sodom and Ammorah, as it was mighty" (Gen.18:2).

Rambam surmises that without these Divine interventions, human creativity would have been irreparably stifled by the actions of that time. Part of the saying "you can't fight city hall" means that social norms can become impossible to change. Rather than allow a game to take a turn for the worse, Hashem must intervene to nurture a better outcome.

Management vs Judgment
None of this is judgment—that comes in the eleventh principle. This, we might call management.

Final judgment must be precise if it is to be just. Management is not final; it is ongoing and adjustable and, therefore, need not be precise.

Management is mentoring and opening up possibilities. If criticism is too harsh, it can be mitigated with pleasantries that come earlier or later. If a new challenge is too overwhelming it can be made easier with new help or better compensation.

A manager's focus is on growth and autonomy. In the best-case scenario, the manager becomes pleasantly surprised by how well the protegè develops. In the worst-case scenario, the manager continues to tweak the situation seeking whatever improvement is possible and never, as Rambam put it, abandoning things.

However, Hashem will not exert control. That would be a logical contradiction to Hashem's goal of individual creativity. The whole universe and all the other players were created, placed, monitored, and juggled just to promote the creativity that each person would muster. Even if it would be only one person. The best Hashem could do is manage the story to maximize our possibilities. Therein lies the reason for life's challenges, to maximize our creative responses. Some maximums only emerge from extreme challenges such as those suffered in a widespread calamity.

Why Widespread Calamities?

Widespread calamities produce two outcomes that trouble us. The most troubling outcome is the death of those who did not deserve to die, the innocent. I shall address this later in the thirteenth and final principle. Other outcomes that are not as final as death, such as loss of wealth, loss of health, loss of relationships, etc., also trouble us because so often they, too, seem undeserved. I answer that disquiet as follows.

The creativity that Hashem is hoping to coax out of us will often not emerge unless we need to overcome something unusual. If it was usual, we would already have a solution. Unusualness is the very thing that elicits creativity. Widespread calamities fit that bill. People don't need to deserve a calamity to justify its appearance. Calamities are just another feature of life that motivates us to succeed, often heroically, where without it we would have just coasted into oblivion.

Understandably, we groan about the tragedies that befall us. But look at it from a different angle. Whatever creative solution we muster will become the center of attention in Hashem's court during our final judgment. That is what Hashem was waiting for! If we were really devastated and prayed—asking Hashem for help to deal with the calamity—the resulting relationship with Hashem will become another court focus, even more fussed over. Final judgment should not be thought of as final retribution but as a final appreciation of what we accomplished.

Answer to: Why Do The Innocent Suffer? Our purpose is to create with our minds as Hashem creates. Our habit, though, is to avoid embracing this potential unless something is making us uncomfortable. That is why Hashem inserts discomforts into the mix, to trigger our creativity.

This is not immediately obvious because if a particular discomfort was directly traceable to our laziness, our choices would be more obvious and less creative. That is why Hashem manages in an invisible way. As for those who didn't need to suffer, Hashem manages to keep things fair by compensating for too much discomfort with extra reward in other areas and the like.

Sometimes, our responses are destructive rather than creative, harming us and others beyond recovery. In those cases, the discomforts Hashem arranges will be specifically designed to alter the course. They will probably be extreme discomforts which then serve double duty by not only altering the course but also by frightening onlookers to behave better so that they never invite similar repercussions.

11 - What Is In It For Me?

The Familiar Ani Ma'amin: I believe with complete faith that the Creator, blessed is His Name, rewards with good those who observe His commandments and punishes those who violate His commandments.

My Critique: This Ani ma'amin treats the subject of reward and punishment as an incentive for good behavior. The World To Come is not mentioned, perhaps because its reputation is too mired in mystery to provide an incentive. Still, this changes Rambam's message which does mention the World To Come. As expounded earlier, Rambam's purpose is to describe reality, so whatever the nature of the reward, he must describe it. Although he does so with the utmost brevity, especially in comparison with his description of Moshe (Chapter 7 above), he still says enough to guide us.

The Yigdal Couplet:

He recompenses man with kindness according to his deed;

He places evil on the wicked according to his wickedness.

My Critique: Aside from inserting a commentary by replacing Rambam's word "reward" with the word "kindness", this adequately reflects Rambam's point.

Rambam's eleventh description of reality: Hashem gives reward to one who performs the commandments of the Torah and punishes one who transgresses its warnings; the big reward is the World To Come and the strong punishment is being cut off. **We have already said enough about this matter.**

The verse that indicates this principle is Moshe's plea, "now, if You will lift up their sin; but if not, erase me please," (Ex.32:32) and Hashem's reply, "The one who sins against Me, I will erase from My book" (Ex.32:33). This is proof that He knows the servant and the sinner to give reward to this one and punishment to that one.

I have already departed from the common understanding of Rambam's tenth statement of the previous chapter so it should come as no surprise that I will do the same here, especially since this and the previous statement are often coupled together. That partially explains why this statement of the Rambam has caused me the most trouble to decipher. The bigger reason, though, is that I suspect this statement caused Rambam the most trouble to compose.

Rambam's Preamble

My suspicion is based on Rambam's lengthy preamble to this list of thirteen descriptions of reality that I have been analyzing. He refers to this preamble when he says, as **bolded** above, "we have already said enough about this matter". I include this preamble for the reader's convenience, but in an appendix rather than the body of my text, because Rambam dismisses most of its content. He seems to have written it to tell us what <u>not</u> to think.

Rambam's list of thirteen was prompted by the Mishnah in Sanhedrin which declares, "all of Israel has a share in the World To Come". This sounds like an incentive through a promise of ultimate reward. In response, Rambam's preamble lengthily describes the various consequences that have been presented through the ages to motivate various audiences, such as unending pleasures that are physical (Garden of Eden) or emotional (Messianic kingdom), or frightening (Gehinnom/Hell). Rambam dismisses each proposal as an oversimplified version of the ultimate World To Come.

(To this day, questions surrounding these concepts continue to bedevil lay people causing most to abandon the thought process. Some just lower their heads and push on, afraid to confront their ignorance, while others weaponize their ignorance into excuses for abandoning religion altogether because they deem it irrational.)

.

Since Rambam's preamble segued into his list of thirteen principles, and since he first digresses to list ten ideas before he returns to the subject of reward and punishment, I conclude his goal was not to describe the World To Come but rather the reality of this world. It must be that we have to be aware of a next world in order to fully understand our current reality. In the process, we may incidentally gain a glimpse of the World To Come (only a glimpse), but the main takeaway is an understanding of this world. As I have been maintaining all along, Rambam's purpose of listing these thirteen ideas is to describe reality—the World To Come is not yet a reality.

That is how I approach this eleventh statement by Rambam. Now, I have to analyze it within that context.

Is Rambam's Proof A Proof?
I begin by analyzing the last part of Rambam's statement: "This is proof that He knows the servant and the sinner to give reward to this one and punishment to that one."—I don't see the proof.

Rambam's proof is a quote from Moshe's plea to Hashem to grant forgiveness for the sin of the golden calf. The day before, about 3,000 people were executed for participating in this sin; then, Moshe informed the rest of the people that, on some level, they too were guilty of a great sin for which he would try to gain their forgiveness. Here are the verses quoted by Rambam:

32. Now, if You will forgive their sin *(chet)* [well and good]; but if not, erase me from the book which You have written!"

33. Hashem said to Moshe, "He who has sinned *(chet)* against Me, I will erase from My book." (Ex. 32:32-33)

Upon first reading, it may appear that Moshe pleaded for forgiveness and got it, but he didn't. Hashem said He will erase those that sinned, not forgive them, and to underscore that message Hashem sent a plague, as reported two verses later. Careful reading uncovers many more questions.

Rambam claimed these verses prove reward and punishment. How?

Which part of Rambam's point does he think these verses address? Reward is not even mentioned! If these verses are quoted to prove punishment for sins, they don't do a very good job of that either because it is only punishing the worst crime of idol worship. Perhaps, other sins are not punished.

Indeed, perhaps they are not. I have been careful to include in the English translation the Hebrew word for sin, namely *chet*. The Torah uses different words to describe bad behavior according to its severity, eg. *pesha* (defiant) and *uvon* (deviant). *Chet* is normally understood as the least bad; it is mistaken behavior, not defiant or deviant behavior.

Chet is the appropriate choice for the sin of the golden calf because the Jewish people couldn't have meant to defy Hashem who had done so much for them. The midrashim tell us they were just desperate for a figurehead to replace Moshe whom they thought had died.

It makes no sense for Hashem to threaten to erase from His book those who sinned with the golden calf because their sin wasn't that bad; they just made a mistake. A *chet* does not deserve the erasure of *korais*.

Furthermore, what was meant by "erase from the book"? They were never in the book anyway. We have no names of those who sinned with the golden calf. On the contrary, others who sinned more grievously are still in the book, such as Amalek, Korech, Bilaam, etc.—not erased.

Unless the book referenced is not the Torah, but rather the book of life, the book of eternity. If so, then Moshe's plea to be erased from the book if Hashem doesn't forgive is too extreme—why should he lose eternal life to save others from the necessary consequences of their actions?

Why would Moshe even think of allowing himself to be erased for eternity? As I noted earlier, when I have a difficult question I keep poking the subject with other questions which usually causes an answer to pop up. My answer popped up from this last question. If Hashem will not forgive the sin of a mistake—just a mistake—then Moshe's whole understanding of Hashem's essence is faulty. In that case, the World To Come would have no value for him because rather than an eternal delight it would be an eternal rebuttal of his entire accomplishment!

But Moshe's perception of Hashem was wholly correct. Of course, Hashem would continue His relationship with the Jewish people, even if it was changed by the mistake of the golden calf. Just like Hashem continued His relationship with Moshe who had also *chet*-sinned by questioning Hashem and would sin again over the water from the rock.

Regarding *chet*, I must point out that *chet*-sin is exactly how we grow in wisdom, self-control, and stature. We think we know what to do, don't seek guidance, and don't listen to it when offered. Instead, we stumble, sometimes injure ourselves but always embarrass ourselves, and, through this, improve ourselves ... somewhat ... it is ongoing.

Having developed these thoughts, another word to revisit in the verse quoted by Rambam is "forgive" for which the Hebrew is *teesa*, carry. When Moshe asks Hashem to forgive the people, it literally means to carry their sin. The commentaries explain that Hashem does actually carry forward the sin of the golden calf, slowly applying its consequences to us all through history. That is a form of forgiveness. It is another way of saying that it changed our relationship with Hashem. That conforms with our own practice. When someone lets us down, then, even after they make amends and we are friends again, we carry forward differently, cautiously.

Given the preceding analysis, it makes better sense to treat Hashem's reply as a rhetorical question, rather than a statement. Not "He who has *chet*-sinned against Me, I will erase from My book", but, **"Will I erase from My book he who has (only) *chet*-sinned against Me?"** No! Hashem will continue to relate and continue to manage, as explained in the previous chapter. But this time on a one-to-one basis.

In fact, let me re-translate because the last chapter was about managing groups and this one is about guaranteeing individuals: "Will I erase from My book any individual who has (only) *chet*-sinned against Me?" Hashem's goal is to create individuals, to give them life, to record them in the book—that is what Hashem calls it. We call it reward.

Taken this way, the reward is implied for almost everyone because how many willfully defy Hashem?

In that case, Rambam has come full circle back to the source of his comment, the Mishnah that proclaimed, "all of Israel has a share in the World To Come". Hashem is managing to include as many of His creations as possible.

A Peek Into *Olam HaBa*

What will the World To Come be like is what we want to know now. Rambam's mention of "reward" (*sachar*) and "big reward" (*sachar gadol*) leads me to some tantalizing insights.

The "big reward" only appears in the World To Come, which makes it mysterious, but its name implies it is only a bigger version of the "reward" in this world which should evoke something familiar. My attempts to reconcile these two opposites of mystery and familiarity led me to examine a feature that could be common to both worlds, namely, the relationships we create.

I explained earlier that Hashem's goal is for us to create like Hashem does, with our minds. What we create with our minds most prolifically, whether we choose to or not, is our relationships. We are driven to do so by our need for physical help, our longing for emotional validity, and our concern for social acceptance. These three drives for physical, emotional, and social stability propel us to create an ever-expanding number of relationships that become intricately intertwined with each other.

But we are so amateurish in these areas that our efforts often create harmful relationships. That establishes the need for the discipline and wisdom of Torah instructions to channel us toward positive relationships. Some relationships are deep, most are not; however, they are all necessary for both us and others.

In this world, we usually recognize the profound value of our deepest relationships. If there persist any clashes within them that we can't seem to resolve we nevertheless plod on because we dare not lose them.

Our other relationships are less deep and less valued, such as with those who live nearby, who provide local services, or who populate our workplace. We need these relationships, too, but value them only modestly and rarely, like the air we breathe. Air is essential and life-affirming, but so much so, and so all-encompassing at the same time, that real appreciation is avoided as too overwhelming.

But what if it wasn't overwhelming? What if, in the case of air, we could trace the benefits of one particular deep breath to the oxygenation of a particular pulse of blood and, from there, to a particular muscle and, from there, to a particular action that we very badly desired to accomplish. Wouldn't that breath then be much more appreciated and marveled at?! It is only our lack of awareness that precludes our appreciation.

Apply the same thinking to a relationship. Suppose we could trace the positive feedback we once gave an occasional acquaintance to their heightened level of self-confidence and, from there, to the convincing impression they made on an investor and, from there, to the financing of a new medical device that conquered cancer and changed the world! Wouldn't that be a delight?! More than a delight, it would be a neverending bragging point.

That possibility shines a light on the teaching, "more attractive is one hour of the spirit's bliss in the World To Come, than all the life of this world (Pirkei Avos 4:22)". Our spirit's bliss in this world is the satisfaction of the contribution we made, but we rarely experience that bliss as deeply as deserved because we cannot trace its full positivity. The Hebrew for "world" is *olam* which also means hidden. In the World To Come, we will become aware of what was previously hidden. "Olam HaBa" (the Hebrew for World To Come) implies "the hidden things will come to us". A new awareness that traces the full extent of our contribution will be so unexpectedly delicious that we can easily imagine how it will outweigh whatever bliss we have had in this world.

Speaking of a neverending bragging point, there wouldn't be any end to their number, either. They would be so prolific that they would merge into each other in the same way individual pixels merge to form an exquisitely nuanced picture of a whole. In the World To Come, our self-image will be a collage of the relationships we formed that finally allowed the World To Come to come. Rambam had to mention the World To Come because it is the natural finale of this world, the coming awareness of what we achieved. The familiar relationships will reveal their mysterious reach, how many benefits did they convey and how many wrong turns did they avert.

As for our deepest relationships, the ones we ploddingly maintained for fear of losing them even as they chafed at us so often, their mystery will also be revealed. The self-effacements that were necessary to preserve them will finally be understood. They were our personal training program to replicate Moshe's model of service to Hashem, to the One who gave us life, our own unique challenge and reward.

A Personal Experience Summarizes

I think I can most easily summarize the above by describing an artifact in my home that I was thinking of as I wrote. I thank my daughter Nechama who made it.

The artifact is a collage of pictures of my kids and grandkids at various stages of their development. It hangs in our kitchen so I pass it quite often. Quite frequently, I stop for a moment to enjoy the memories. Not really the memories because nothing specific comes to mind, it is rather just the awareness of our connections with each other. It is a heartful and warming enjoyment that lasts and lasts.

I guess I am reflecting on the family my wife and I built and continue to nurture which is to say, relate to. These reflections made me realize that "family" is just the tip of the iceberg we can see and, so, mount in a frame. As the cliche teaches, most of the iceberg floats below the surface. There are innumerably more relationships we have built over the years but don't feel entitled to mount in a frame. Why not? Perhaps, in this life, it would be too presumptuous to claim influence. (That may be why I never thought of making the collage of pictures that my daughter did.)

But, in the World To Come, Hashem will reward us with full awareness about all our other relationships, how we helped, challenged, and inspired; then, we will learn the full extent of our influence. That would constitute a beautiful collage in an exquisite frame upon which we would never tire of gazing. Not available any other way.

What About Here & Now?

Read again Rambam's statement here. It first confirms reward and punishment in this world, not only the next. Many disbelieve this because they observe so many obviously righteous people suffering and so many wicked people flourishing. In fact, this makes them disbelieve the World To Come, too.

My answer to them is that Rambam does not say only the pious enjoy happy lives and only the wicked suffer. I have already explained that Hashem's creativity necessitates a wide range of scenarios in which to place us. Some are destined to live comfortably and some are not. Similarly, some are created with pious tendencies and some are not. All these and other variables provide each human with a unique testing environment that allows each to earn uniquely personal rewards and punishments.

Because these variables appear in unique groupings, we will never have enough experience in this world to distinguish between what is reward and punishment and what is the testing environment—not for others and not for ourselves. That is why Rambam has to assure us of the cause-effect nature of mitzvah-reward. Our inability to distinguish is also why Hashem provided the Torah to guide us to success.

For example, consider two people who seek to help charities. One will be granted unusual economic success so that he will be able to donate generously. Such success is not a reward for the person's donations but rather a test to measure their generosity. Granted, there is joy in giving, in being able to give, and joy afterward, if you are able to see the good that came of your gift. But, the joy, itself, might be a test to see if it excuses further giving.

The other person with the same selfless desire to donate to charity might not be as rich as the person described above. Every time this second person donates, the amount is much lower and is accompanied by embarrassment and/or frustration for not doing more. His after-death reward will be equal to the reward for the first person because they both did all that they could. The second person might even be rewarded more to compensate for the embarrassment and/or frustration he endured in this world.

Any Rewards For Non-Religious Behavior?

Rambam only mentions rewards and punishment as a consequence of religious behavior. Are there any rewards for good behavior outside of following the commandments? What about all the positive behaviors that are <u>not</u> traceable back to the commandments? There are many Jewish people who are kind, generous, and loving human beings, but not religious. There are others who improve the whole world such as by inventing a life-saving device and the like. Will they not receive a reward for their righteousness or life-changing contribution?

To formulate an answer, I asked myself: What kind of reward would such people appreciate? Probably, kind, generous, and loving human beings would most enjoy reciprocal behavior from the people with whom they interact. People would love them back. Not everybody because then it would be too cheap. You can't be best friends with everybody because then nobody is a best friend. Similarly, for the life-saving inventor the best reward would be success, it works. But not success easily found or developed because then everybody would be able to do it.

In other words, into every life some rain must fall, otherwise, nothing would be appreciated. So there are rewards but they have to be earned to be considered valuable. Having said that, "reward" is the wrong word to use because it implies something extra beyond the expected consequence. Such is not the case here. People who are nice can reasonably expect others to reciprocate and people who invent a cost-effective solution to a persistent problem will be applauded for their success. These consequences are part of reality but Rambam did not have to include them in his description of reality since they are already well known.

Any Rewards For A Little Religious Behavior?

Some earn rewards only in this world, nothing in the next. This can occur when a person has miserably failed their potential in this world but has still managed to do one or two things right. Hashem's fairness mandates a reward for those one or two things, so such people are rewarded in this world with wealth, fame, power, or whatever. It looks like they are getting treasures, but really, such things are trivial in comparison to the reward of eternal satisfaction available after death. Indeed, the recipients are always seeking more, so how satisfying can these "treasures" be?

As for final punishment, here is why Rambam describes the punishment for one who has miserably failed their potential in this world as being "cut off". If such a person retained awareness after death, what would that awareness be? It would be the realization that they had failed miserably. No longer suspected, but confirmed, they amounted to nothing. Can there be any more devastating experience? Certainly not, especially since it would last forever. Better for Hashem to just erase that person's identity from the memory banks, "cut off" in the language of old.

Leaving the world in better shape
One last conclusion emerges from this discussion. The real goal of life is not to fix this world. Hashem can run the world very well without our help and despite our mistakes, thank you very much. The goal is to create ourselves. World problems are just a context, maybe a pretext, for doing so.

Another pretext for creating ourselves is our own nagging sense of unique destiny. Since birth, our parents have praised how special we are or complained how unusual we are (you know who you are:). Science joined the chorus by discovering our unique fingerprints and more recently our unique DNA. It seems as time goes on and the population increases, Hashem has to provide us with more and more assurances of this, eg. iris recognition and voice identification. Not a problem because Hashem has no limits, so there are no limits on the range of possible human creations.

Correspondingly, there is no limit to Hashem's fascination to see, monitor, and hopefully (from our perspective) enjoy the creative choices we each make.

That enjoyment must be predicated on the fulfillment of everything Hashem created. It can't be that just one or two things turned out correctly or even one million or two million things turned out correctly. That is too limited a purview for Hashem. It has to be everything. The next thing to discover is how Hashem ensures it all comes together.

Answer to: What Is In It For Me? "Me" is in it for me. Being just a mental image created by Hashem, we live with the subconscious fear that we don't matter. A reward would disprove that, it would show we are valued. But the reward would have to fit what we consider real.

If the only reality we have developed for ourselves is the reality we know here, then the reward will have to be a this-world type. That is not comparable to what could have been but a this-world reward is all that will satisfy us. So, that is what we will get.

If, instead, and this is what Hashem plans for, we took tenuous steps beyond what was immediately visible into a reality we created with our mind, through our Torah learning and behavior control, then the reward will be the confirmation of that reality, the fulfillment of that self. The exquisiteness of that reward will be out-of-this-world.

The distinction between this-world-rewards and after-death-rewards leads to a deeper appreciation of the reality at stake. After-death-rewards require life-after-death and that life must be qualitatively different from the life we know. That life must be so much more expansive—if only for the fact that death is no longer possible. Prophets have been unable to describe it, not because of their shortcomings but because of ours. What they were able to say was: one moment of life after death provides more pleasure than all the pleasures ever experienced by everyone in this world—for all time.

The only way I can imagine that to be true is if our awareness after death confirmed unequivocally the value of all we had achieved in this world, all the creativity, all the harmonization with others, all the value we had added to Hashem by following the instructions. Such sublime confirmation of our identity and life's work is what we have always sought. It must entail pleasure without limit!

(I further imagine that it will segue somehow into further creative achievements in a life-to-come using the powers we developed in this life. I imagine this because the very nature of life is growth. How can we grow further? So many possibilities could be. Perhaps, in addition to our three-dimensional world of length, width and height, we will grapple with an additional three dimensions such as energy, determination (will power) and personality (man/woman). Such speculation is obviously beyond this discussion—Hashem has no limits!)

12 - Are We On The Right Track?

<u>The Familiar Ani Ma'amin</u>: I believe with complete faith in the coming of the Mashiach, and even though he may delay, nevertheless I anticipate every day that he will come.

My Critique: This is a fair condensation of Rambam's point although, to my mind, it does add one troublesome idea, that of a daily anticipation of Mashiach's arrival—Rambam did not say that. Since most days Mashiach's arrival does not appear very likely, anticipating that it could happen immediately lends it a magical quality. That conflicts with my theme of reality. My theme will still work, though, if the anticipation is not for the full salvation we expect, only it's dawning, as I shall explain.

<u>The Yigdal Couplet</u>:
By the End of Days He will send our Mashiach,
to redeem those longing for His final salvation.

My Critique: This adequately reflects Rambam's point.

> **Rambam's twelfth description of reality:** There will be a Messianic era. One must maintain the conviction that he will come and not consider him

late. If he tarries, wait for him and do not set him a deadline nor predict from any verses the time of his coming. The sages said, "Curse those who calculate the end" (Sanhedrin 97b).

Expect the Mashiach will have great advantage and stature and honor above all of the kings that ever were; as all prophesied about him, from Moshe to Malachi. One who doubts him or his future stature denies the Torah, as the Torah testifies about him in *Parshat Bilaam* and in *Parshat Atem Nitzavim*.

Included in this principle is that there should not be a king in Israel except from the House of David descended through Shlomo alone. Anyone who disputes the status of this family denies the name of Hashem and the words of His prophets.

Who is Mashiach?

As developed in previous chapters, Hashem's end goal is to nurture the greatest possible creative growth of each person. Part of the creative aspect is the unique struggle in which every person must engage to fully and finally express themselves.

Some struggle against the limits of poverty, others do the opposite, they struggle against the distraction of riches; some can't focus because they are dull-minded, others can't focus because their wit is too quick; some suffer ill health, others abuse good health; some endure social upheaval, others social apathy; and on and on and on. Whatever the struggle, it reminds us we are flawed creatures, unsure of how to find satisfaction. We have Torah but we still need help—help of a Biblical proportion.

Enter Mashiach (Messiah is a poor transliteration of this Hebrew word). He will be a leader with the charisma and depth to turn the entire world in the proper direction. Not with miracles that override our creative freedoms, but with an unusual talent for harnessing our creativity. He need not be a prophet but he might be one, although not a greater one than Moshe. As explained earlier, no one will ever surpass Moshe's clarity. All clarity that is humanly possible was embedded by Moshe into the Torah as if dictated by Hashem word for word. That wisdom will be unlocked by the Mashiach so that we can apply it to our circumstances. This is the failsafe mechanism that will kick in at the end of days for us to transition to the World To Come.

Mashiach literally means "anointed one" because he will be a descendant of Kings David and Shlomo and will be anointed with holy oil as they were. In addition to that prerequisite, Rambam reports (Laws of Kings and Their Battles 11:4) that he will be a learned scholar and a pious practitioner of Torah instructions. If such a man arises and is able to persuade all the people of Israel to follow the Torah and strengthen their observance, waging the battles of Hashem as necessary, then we can assume this man is Mashiach, but only temporarily.

There have been several men of such temporary stature over the generations but never one who was able to complete the confirmation. In order to be confirmed, Mashiach needs to succeed in two critical endeavors: one, rebuilding the Temple in Jerusalem, and two, attracting the exiled Jewish people back to Israel. Failure to reach these two final levels of success before dying would prove that, retroactively, he never was Mashiach.

Once the Temple is rebuilt, we will once again fulfill long-dormant Biblical instructions such as sacrifices, Sabbatical and Jubilee years, and cities of refuge within expanded borders.

All of the above will be accomplished under the same laws of science that govern us now. We will continue to need food, drink, rest, friends, teachers, and mentors. Mashiach need not prophesize nor perform miracles. Nevertheless, his influence will extend beyond Israel, bringing all of humanity to live the reality expressed by the Torah. It will be a golden age for humanity. The above defines the original Jewish idea of Mashiach.

Why is Mashiach Necessary?

It can't transpire that everyone will grow on their own into a clear perception of Hashem's reality because Hashem's creativity has always produced a wide range of human potential. The wide range means that many people will be unable to perfect themselves until they are inspired by a dynamic leader. It is not uncommon for inspiring leaders to coax their followers into extraordinary accomplishments. However, a prerequisite is the conviction that it can be done.

People who despair of that possibility give up. They say, "If it will never happen, what is the point in trying?" This defeats Hashem's plan of cajoling every individual to twist and turn in constant pursuit of their own satisfying contribution. Twisting and turning, trial and error, that is what it calls for, and for a lifetime. Unique contributions cannot be accomplished overnight like a homework assignment. They are a lifetime assignment. To stay the course we need to live with the hope of final success. Mashiach is the embodiment of that final success.

The best kind of hope is the hope that we can achieve the goal ourselves. That is true; we can definitely improve ourselves enough to justify Mashiach's arrival. But, given our freedom of choice, we may never do so. In that case, tradition tells us that Hashem will send Mashiach anyway by a certain, final deadline. Now, human nature being what it is, if we knew that deadline and it was very far off, we would take our time in trying to bring Mashiach sooner. "We still have time", we would say. For the sake of motivating us to do the best we can, as soon as we can, it is prohibited to predict the deadline for Mashiach's arrival.

Why Hereditary Positions?

Rambam made a point of saying that Mashiach would be a descendant of Kings David and Shlomo. Today, many would argue against hereditary positions of power. When the time comes, we prefer to select a leader based on ability. Be aware, this has not been past practice, usually because the family in power had the resources to stay in power.

Past practice was probably also a consequence of the population's acceptance of the divine right of kings, namely the belief that Hashem selected this family for royalty and so might punish any people who rebelled. The origin of this idea probably came from Hashem's promise to David that all future kings would descend from him. Although that promise was contingent on David's descendants being worthy, subsequent heirs no doubt suppressed that detail.

The Hereditary Nature Of The Chosen People

Stronger evidence of Hashem's preference for hereditary positions comes from the idea of the chosen people. Since this is part of the Torah reality that I am trying to describe, it deserves some airing especially since the idea of a chosen people bothers many.

First, the Jewish people didn't ask to be chosen. In fact, the many times that the Jews in the wilderness complained and threatened to return to Egypt can be taken as evidence that they preferred to not be chosen, to be left normal like everybody else. The chosenness was a piece of news delivered by the prophet Moshe and preserved in the Torah over which they had no editorial control, as described in the chapters above.

Second, hereditary qualities should not offend. No one gets morally outraged to learn that there is such a thing as a hereditary disease. It is just another one of those facts that we have to deal with like skin color, baldness, body size, and the like.

A more sensitive soul can easily be another hereditary feature, one that requires extra restrictions. That is what the chosenness seems to imply—the need for extra restrictions. Accordingly, Jewish people have to watch their diet more closely (via kosher) and abstain from personal pursuits more often (via Shabbos and Yom Tov regulations). These are but two examples of serious restrictions.

In Temple times, the kohens, another hereditary position of chosenness, were even more restricted. They were never given their own land, so instead, had to rely on tithes of produce from non-kohens. Once received, these tithes had to be consumed in a state of spiritual purification. Spiritual purity required them to be constantly aware of their environment, similar to the level of care that doctors must exercise to remain germ-free—not a relaxed state of mind.

Heredity is just part of Hashem's method of securing a vast array of creative outputs. Every individual is given a particular bundle of skills, talents, shortcomings, and handicaps with the goal of eliciting a creative response, or better, many creative responses.

To further shape unique responses, same or similar bundles skills, talents, shortcomings, etc. can be allocated to individuals who are members of different groups with different histories, different yearnings, and so on. On an absolute scale, some will excel much more than others and some will falter much more. But on the more important scale of relativity, Hashem could easily value more the one who faltered than the one who excelled, when the faltering was much less than expected given the handicaps imposed, and the excelling was hardly enough to justify all the advantages granted.

Why Mention Both David and Shlomo?

Rambam also made a point of saying Mashiach would be a descendant of both Kings David and Shlomo. Why wasn't it enough to mention just David, which is usually the way it is expressed? I have an eyebrow-raising observation to publicize on this subject, as follows. The genealogy of the Mashiach includes a repeated history of sexual innuendo. Not sexual misconduct, mind you—that would have aborted the process—but innuendo.

It starts with Lot, Abraham's nephew. **Lot and his daughters** (Gen. 19) were the only ones saved from the destruction of Sodom and Gomorrah. His daughters, thinking they were the only remaining humans on the planet, impregnated themselves through their father, after getting him drunk so he wouldn't realize the debasement. They did this for the noble purpose of propagating the human race, so it wasn't a sin. But, it put a skeleton in the closet. One of the children born from this incident was Moav, the ancestor of Ruth who was the great-grandmother of David.

The sexual innuendo continues with **the story of Tamar** (Gen.38). She married into the family of Yehuda, father of the tribe. Her widowhood eventually prompted her to disguise herself as a prostitute and trick Yehuda into a moment of intimacy which resulted in the birth of the ancestor of David. The prostitute disguise wagged a lot of tongues about a skeleton in the closet but Tamar was completely within her rights to build a family through Yehuda.

Generations later, a Moabite woman decided to convert to Judaism out of devotion to the faith, as related in the **Book of Ruth**. This created a bit of a scandal because Ruth was the first Moabite to ever convert and the Torah seemed to prohibit it. Boaz, a renowned leader and scholar, applied a careful reading of the Torah to prove that the prohibition only extended to Moabite men, not Moabite women. Accordingly, Boaz, a descendant of Tamar, was able to convince the court that he was permitted to marry Ruth, a descendant of Lot. David was their great-grandson.

The Moabite scandal did not disappear, though. Closet skeletons were piling up and doubts lingered even in the mind of their grandson, **Yishai, David's father**. These doubts were never reported in the text but were at the heart of a curious estrangement between David and his family (1 Samuel 16:6-13 and 17:28). Even after the prophet had announced to David's family that he was to be the future king, they continued to keep their distance from him. Why?

The strange story that explains this was preserved in the oral tradition, as reported in *The Book Of Our Heritage* (Feldheim Books, 1978). Yishai, an extraordinarily devout man, worried that he might not really qualify as a full Jew because of the Moabite lineage of his great-grandmother, Ruth. Maybe his great-grandfather, Boaz, had made a mistake. As a precaution, Yishai separated from his native-born Jewish wife. He did not divorce her, though, because his suspicions might be mistaken, making divorce the wrong thing to do—I warned you that he was extraordinarily devout.

Due to the mitzvah to procreate and the permissibility of a second wife, at that time, Yishai consecrated a maidservant with a condition that would satisfy all the legal technicalities, as follows: "If I am a native Jew then I free you from your maidservant status; that makes you a full Jewess and my legal second wife (polygamy was permissible and common back then); if I am not permitted to marry a Jewish woman, then you remain a maidservant and my relations with you are permitted because I am descended from a Moabite convert". (This legal construction, by the way, qualifies as a creative act, of the kind which Hashem desires from us.)

Thereafter, Yishai was only intimate with the maidservant. His wife, however, realized that Yishai's suspicions about his ancestry were ill-founded and bemoaned her separation from her husband. The maidservant, also devout if only from the prevailing zeitgeist within the home, felt bad for her mistress and suggested to Yishai's wife that she take her place in the marital chamber one night, which she did. From that night's intimacy, Yishai's wife became pregnant with David but Yishai never realized he was the father. Consequently, he concluded that his wife had committed adultery with another man and considered David an illegitimate *mamzer* child. Not David's fault, of course, but not accrediting him with a choice legacy, either. Count yet another skeleton in the closet.

Thus began David's career, under a cloud. It seemed to be always so, as when he had to flee from Shaul, his predecessor, and all his other enemies, and even from rebellion within his own family. In the middle of all this, **David committed his own act of indiscretion with Batsheva**. But, it wasn't as bad as the text implies (2 Samuel 11), as follows.

Batsheva's husband was in the army which was at war. The prevailing practice was to divorce one's wife before going to war, lest the husband disappears through death or capture, leaving the spouse in the terrible doubt of being widowed or not. Thus, even though Batsheva had been married, she was now a divorcee when David happened to see her bathing on the rooftop. David, as devout as his father Yishai, was the opposite of a peeping tom, nearer to being a prophet. He interpreted the accidental viewing of a bathing woman as a sign from Hashem to marry her. David was right and their child turned out to be King Shlomo but due to his insensitivity in the way he went about it, he was punished. Count another instance of sexual innuendo on the way to the Mashiach.

Finally, there was **Shlomo himself whose fame was partially founded on the number of wives** he took (Kings I 11). The Torah allows polygamy but warns kings not to marry too many wives because they will turn his heart to idol worship. King Shlomo, the wisest man ever, allowed himself to marry too many wives because he was so careful not to worship idols. The wisest man ever was duped by sex into thinking he could outsmart the Torah! If the Torah predicted a result, it was bound to happen and it did. (Note: The oral tradition insists Shlomo never worshiped idols—he never could have been considered the wisest man if he had—but his foreign-born wives did and for that, he was personally responsible.)

Six Steps Of Creation
All in all, there were six instances of sexual innuendo leading up to the promised messianic destiny. Lot and his daughter first, Yehudah and Tamar second, Ruth and Boaz third, Yishai sireing David fourth, David and Batsheva fifth, and Shlomo sixth.

Had Rambam only mentioned David, I might have thought the Mashiach legacy had been earned somehow by David alone. The double mention of David and Shlomo made me analyze the history which then brought to light the common thread of sexual innuendo.

Why in the world would sexual innuendo be the necessary backdrop to the messianic idea? There were six incidents, one for each day of creation. This world was created with the plan of eventually reaching Mashiach. That was the end, what was the start? Hashem created man to create. The first mitzvah deployed the sex drive as the initial push in that direction. "Be fruitful and multiply" is a physical act that leads to creating new people who are, essentially, new ideas or new sources of ideas.

But, as explained above, creativity can be wrong-headed and destructive. Best if we learn how to control that ourselves. The Mashiach is the leader who will usher in a golden age of managing creativity to keep it positive. The guidelines for positive creativity are collectively called the Torah. It is as if these guidelines draw a line in the sand. Up to here is positive creativity, beyond the line it is negative. Mashiach is the best one to teach us to stay within the lines because his hereditary qualifications depended on it. That is why I called it sexual innuendo and not sexual misconduct—it stayed just within the letter of the law but, because it was so close to the line, innuendo was stirred.

How Will It Work Today?

As in all human endeavors, Mashiach will need helpers and supporters to disseminate the proper teachings and guidance. This is and always has been the function of the Jewish people on the world stage. Not for self-aggrandizement but simply as friendly service people who want to help, who enjoy helping and who know how to help.

What is surprising is that the messianic operation will be centralized in Israel. I would have thought that the vibrant Jewish communities that have blossomed around the world would provide a wider platform from which to spread the teachings worldwide.

Another surprise is the insistence on reintroducing animal sacrifices as an integral part of the Temple service. My impression is that a lot of people will consider that to be a step backward.

Pondering these issues brought to mind another question. If Mashiach is so successful in spreading Torah wisdom to all people, wouldn't everyone want to convert to Judaism? And then wouldn't he have to bring them all to Israel? That doesn't sound right but it leads to an insight that paints a more realistic picture.

Animal Sacrifices In Israel, Something Else Elsewhere

Temple service is not for all Jews, only for the kohens. Most of the Temple site is forbidden entry to non-kohens and most of the sacrificial activities are performed by the kohens out of sight of anyone else. Even the kohens are absent from the Temple most of the year because they take turns working in the temple, only one week every twenty-four weeks, basically two weeks a year. The rest of the time, their mandate is to learn and teach Torah to the rest of the population. Like the animals they sacrifice, they sacrifice their normal human yearnings to exemplify Torah behavior and wisdom for the benefit of all. The message of animal sacrifice may be more directed at them.

Their income consists of tithes from everyone else. That might not be feasible if only part of the world's Jewish population was present. Manna will not fall from heaven. Non-kohen Jews will still have to farm the land and produce other wealth in the normal manner. The more Jews in Israel producing wealth, the better they will be able to sustain their spiritual mentors.

Animal sacrifices don't inspire everybody. That is ok because nothing inspires everybody. But everybody can be inspired. If all the vibrant, Jewish communities from around the world can be transplanted with their talents, resources, languages, and customs, and then reconfigured and integrated into Israeli society (something they have been practicing and doing since the establishment of the modern state) then that will serve as an inspiring model for every country how they can create their relationship with Hashem, according to their resources, which are different than those in Israel.

The Silver Lining of the CoronaVirus

The coronavirus has taught everyone to connect electronically. The tools were there before but they were being used not nearly as much, despite the pent-up concern for the environment. Computers consume a lot less energy than cars, planes, and other means of travel and spew off no visible pollution. Nevertheless, it took a virus to persuade people to change their behavior.

This could be cited as an example of how Hashem reacts to our actions or lack thereof to stimulate us towards creative solutions. Now that we have become more accustomed to communicating electronically, it is easier to see how the Jewish people could teach and guide other peoples from their headquarters in Israel. Israel, itself, with its many transplanted communities, will be a powerhouse model for how to do it.

Perhaps, facilitating outreach from Israel will turn out to have been Hashem's hidden agenda in bringing the virus. But however the messianic age unfolds, it will work. Hashem will coax it to work without removing our free-willed creativity.

Not all the required pieces are in place, yet. Perhaps, we will finally learn how to employ our brains fully. Perhaps, we will discover a drug that will open our brain to fuller usage. The point is, we can each do more. Science has proven that! We just haven't yet found a scientific way to implement a golden age. Mashiach will act as a booster shot to maximize our human potential.

Answer to: Are We On The Right Track? Of course, we are on the right track! Hashem has made sure of that all through history, as discussed in Chapter 10, and many righteous people have contributed along the way.

The better question is, are <u>we contributing</u> to this track? There are many signs that indicate we are and these encourage us to continue. The most visible is the return from exile and the triumph of the modern state of Israel—sure evidence of the hand of Hashem helping us gain unprecedented achievements.

Why is Hashem helping so much now? I think it is due to the unprecedented vibrancy of Jewish scholarship around the world, despite the many lures of materialism gone wild. No one will be able to trace this but we can rarely trace Hashem's imprint because, remember, Hashem desires to remain invisible. Why? Maybe because if Hashem was visible, everything would be certain. While Hashem is invisible, we cannot be certain, we have to hope.

Hope is something only we can create. Mashiach is a realistic picture of what that hope can be.

13 - What About Those Who Never Had A Chance?

The Familiar Ani Ma'amin: I believe with complete faith that there will be a resuscitation of the dead whenever the wish emanates from the Creator, blessed is His Name, and exalted is His mention forever and for all eternity.

My Critique: This hardly condenses Rambam's point, but does represent it fairly. Rambam's brevity affords me an opportunity to creatively fill some gaps, as shall soon become apparent.

The Yiqdal Couplet:

God will revive the dead in His abundant kindness – Blessed forever is His praised Name.

My Critique: This adequately reflects Rambam's point.

The thirteenth description of reality: The Revival of the dead and we have already elucidated it.

What Were You Expecting?

Christians call it Heaven, Muslims call it Paradise, Buddhists call it Nirvana and Jews call it the World To Come. Each religion envisions it differently but all agree there is a new life after death. Some interpret this last of Rambam's thirteen points to be referring to that new life. The reason Rambam doesn't say much about it is because it is indescribable, they explain.

I agree that the World To Come will provide indescribable pleasure; I must agree because of the authoritative statement in Pirkei Avos. There the sages set the pace for brief descriptions of the World To Come with the curt "one moment there [in the World To Come] is equal to all the pleasures ever experienced by everybody in this world" (PA 4:17).

This assertion describes a pleasure different from the one commonly anticipated. Many envision heaven as a place where each can pursue their favorite pastimes forever. The pleasures are ones with which we are familiar and the bonus lies in how long they last — forever. The sages could have easily described it as such, but they didn't. Instead, "one moment in the next world equal to all the moments in this world" suggests pleasure of a different magnitude than physical. The sages have alerted us that physical pleasures will no longer be attractive after the death of the body; such pleasures won't even exist.

Some more sophisticated minds might envision a hitherto never experienced spiritual delight. As if Hashem would say, "here, because you were so well-behaved, enjoy this wave of delight that I wash over you". But this would be artificial, not a natural outcome of everything we had done up to then. If such an unnatural outcome was satisfactory, then why not award it from the outset? Why burden us with so much pain beforehand?

A Different Expectation

The above questions drove me to suggest my concept of the final reward in the way I did in Chapter 11, which I repeat here: The only way I can imagine a moment of awareness after death will convey more pleasure to an individual than all the pleasures ever experienced by anyone in this life is if it confirmed unequivocally the value of all the person had achieved in this world, all the creativity, all the harmonization with others, and all the satisfaction the person gave Hashem by following the instructions.

Anyone who has ever pleased a parent by making him or her proud has had a modest taste of this pleasure. Such sublime confirmation of our identity and life's work is what we have always sought. It must entail pleasure without limit!

I further imagine it will segue into further creative achievements in a life-to-come using the powers we developed in this life, consistent with Hashem's everlasting focus on creativity. I cannot imagine anything less because life, by definition, cannot be static; it must embrace change.

Whether the above offers a clearer insight or not into the World To Come, the fact that Rambam mentioned it explicitly in Chapter 11, and not here, suggests that it is not the subject of this thirteenth point. Nor should it be. My understanding is that Rambam's thirteen points describe the key features of reality. The World To Come is a different reality, it is a world not yet here. There is no doubt it is coming but only deserves mention in terms of this world, namely, reward and punishment consequences of behavior here, as Rambam mentioned explicitly in Chapter 11.

What then is Rambam describing here with the resurrection of the dead? Just simply that people who have died will come back to life, to this world. The reason there is so little description of this point is that there was no need for Rambam to describe this resurrected life—we already know life in this world.

Why Resurrect The Dead?
The real question to answer is: What essential part of reality does this describe that requires the thirteenth point? The previous point, Mashiach, introduced into Rambam's portrait of reality the element of hope. We have to live with hope, otherwise, we despair. We get depressed and self-destruct—the exact opposite of

Hashem's desire—rather than create. That is why Rambam had to add the Mashiach point after reward and punishment. Now, what does the resurrection of the dead add to Rambam's portrait of reality?

I mentioned before that Hashem wants to be fair. Hashem can do whatever Hashem wants, fair or not. Of course. But Hashem wants to have a relationship with us. That requires our willing participation which can only happen if Hashem is seen as fair. That is why even the wicked get some sort of reward for the paltry good they accomplished. It is a hallmark of Hashem's fairness. If Hashem was not fair, we would abandon the relationship. The whole crux of a relationship is that we have an agreed rate of exchange between us, whether it be an exchange of product, service, ideas, or time spent. "Fair" is a one-word description of an agreement to relate.

In my Chapter 12 examination of the Mashiach concept, I expounded on the magnificent booster shot that everybody will receive at that time. By virtue of Mashiach's leadership, everybody will be primed to relate to Hashem.

People alive then will still have to put in the effort but, when they do, the payoff will be astounding. It will be similar to opening a business in an area where they just struck gold—everybody does well. Carrying this analogy further, when such business people finally retire, they will be able to do so in style, having all the resources they need.

Similarly, people who live during Mashiach's leadership will be able to relate to Hashem so much better, in terms of wisdom and attitude and self-control, that they will be primed to appreciate and enjoy their new life in the World To Come. Such people will be ready to retire from this life and start a new one.

But what about all the people who died before Mashiach arrived? Many of them lived through terrible times that prevented almost any kind of spiritual achievement. Such people won't have discovered reality to much of any degree—how will they relate to Hashem?

The answer is that their original life was only to test whether they deserve to get a second chance. Did they make sufficient use of the meager opportunities pre-Mashiach times offered? If so, then they deserve a second round that will afford them maximum opportunity for personal growth. They will come alive again in the messianic era armed with a talent that others won't have—the talent of squeezing the most out of the least. Under Mashiach's leadership, they will be able to grow as much as anyone else ever could. It is only fair because they will need, as we all do, tremendous preparation to relate to Hashem, the creator of all.

The same answer applies to those who died in widespread calamities. Earlier, I promised to answer how Hashem could allow innocent people to die in such an accidental way. It didn't seem feasible to conclude that all caught in a flood, fire, or airplane crash deserved to die. Such calamities don't trouble us so badly when there is another side to the coin. A second life in a better time would balance out a lot of inequities.

This is not to deny the numerous painful repercussions that accompany the death of the innocent. The repercussions are usually immeasurable—how much more so when death happens without warning. However, this is just the worst example of a well known fact: life is regularly full of painful events. In the end, the only idea that makes such events bearable is the conviction that fairness will prevail in the end. The promise of the dead coming back to life again offers this possibility of fairness ultimately prevailing.

Compare To Near-Death Experiences

But is it fair to the dead? Wouldn't the dead have already become close to Hashem after death and then not want to come back to this life with all its doubts and challenges? There is a whole genre of literature and Youtube videos by people who have had NDE which stands for near-death experiences. The "near-death" title is a little misleading because, for a while, they were clinically dead, not nearly. Estimates are that it has happened to millions of people currently alive.

After the NDE, most remember experiencing Hashem (by whatever name was familiar) who bathed them with such overwhelming love, acceptance, and a feeling of well-being that they loathed leaving it behind in order to come back to life. Some identify that experience as a return to the Garden of Eden, a way station before the advent of the final World To Come. If that same Garden of Eden experience is being enjoyed by those who have died and not come back to life, would it be fair now to yank them back here, away from that beautiful experience?

One answer may be that the beautiful NDE is only experienced by those destined to come back immediately. Maybe those destined to stay dead and come back later feel nothing while dead. When they come back, they won't even realize that they have been dead. It will be like the feeling when regaining consciousness after being anesthetized. I have been anesthetized so I can testify to those who haven't had the experience—it is not like waking up from sleep. Upon waking up from sleep, you realize some time has elapsed. In contrast, regaining consciousness from being "under" gives no feeling of time elapsing; in fact, it takes some evidence to convince you otherwise. Maybe, waking up from the dead will be the same sensation.

Waking up from being "under" might be the most appropriate sensation for those who died achievement-less because self-awareness while dead would not have brought any joy of accomplishment. Nor sorrow or punishment. Their lack of achievement was through no fault of their own, circumstances just didn't allow much. But since they did manage not to corrupt themselves too badly, while alive, coming back makes it fair. They get a second chance.

Some who don't need a second chance might come back, too, to mentor and help. Although, they did achieve much and did enjoy the consequent self-awareness, they might be willing to come back for the sake of helping others, even though that requires something like a fifteen-yard penalty—I am pulling in an analogy from the game of football here. It would be worth it for them to once again exercise the altruism they developed in themselves.

This very goal — helping others realize the ultimate truths — might explain why Hashem gives some people near-death experiences. These people certainly publicize their positive experiences which let others get a hint of their reward to come. On the other hand, these NDE reports haven't revolutionized our thinking or behavior even though there are so many (between 4 to 15% of the population). Perhaps, they are just setting the groundwork. Perhaps, others who have been dead for some time and accumulated intimate awareness of Hashem while dead will also come back and, based on the groundwork of the NDE's, be able to teach and convince others of the right messages.

Reincarnation - A Completely Different Scenario

The foregoing scenario is predicated on the sudden coming-back-to-life of people who have been long dead. Some people ask, at what age will the dead be resurrected? Will they come back at the age that they died or in the prime of life? Some ask, will they come back naked or clothed? I am not sure if these are facetious questions by the scoffers or innocent questions by the naive.

People coming back to life will be a miracle of the highest order! We will all be stunned beyond question! The whole world will be in shock and quite ready to undertake whatever belief and behavior a compelling leader will promote. That leader must be the real Mashiach because Hashem would not bring back the dead to allow a false Mashiach to succeed.

Or, the resurrection may take place after the time of Mashiach's leadership, at a time when all humanity has already committed itself to the proper pursuit of Torah knowledge, worship, and behavior. Then, the resurrection will no longer be a surprise of any kind.

People will be waiting for it and will be primed to guide the newly resurrected into Torah observance just as everyone else has already done. Now the resurrected will get their second chance, but this time in an environment supporting their spiritual success. Everyone helping each other grow in Torah knowledge and practice will be the crowning glory of the Messianic age.

Or, maybe the resurrection will not be noticeable at all. That possibility could occur if resurrection takes place by having the soul of the dead be reborn as a new baby. There is a mention of such in Kabbalah called *Gilgul* which literally means rolling over—the soul rolls over from one body to another. In other circles, it is called reincarnation. There is some evidence of this already occurring—some people describe events of past lives, either through hypnosis or other mind-altering procedures.

Under this scenario, the former life is a subconscious memory within the newborn, to be brought forward into conscious memory at some point, or not. This could qualify as a resurrection and a fair shot at a second chance according to the following criteria. Each human is conceived by Hashem as a package of abilities and disabilities, in a uniquely different formula from all others. Each formula is tasked with the mandate to become the best possible creator that it can, 2nd-level to Hashem as described above in Chapter 5.

Some formula packages (by that I mean humans) will fail to create enough to qualify for the World To Come. An abject failure means the "formula" deserves to be totally erased from the "database" as a failed experiment. A lesser failure means the "formula" was close enough to passing to get resurrected as a different human for a second chance. The fact that second-chance humans may never remember most of their past life, if any part at all, does not make them substantially different from everyone else. After all, "what did you have for breakfast this morning?" will make you realize that you have long forgotten the majority of your days.

Most of life is forgettable. The key memories are the ones that created something for us, a new insight, a new determination, a new talent. Those will always come to the fore and constitute our eternal pride and self-affirmation in the World To Come.

A cautionary note. We will also remember the things we destroyed. If one has too many such memories, that person won't want to be in the World To Come—too many painful memories. The result will be the cut-off status discussed in Chapter 11—the person will cease to be. If one has just a relatively few such memories, that person will suffer bouts of shame until adjusting to the less-than-perfect position he or she occupies—as we do here.

Answer to: What About The Guys That Never Had A Chance? Easy. They will get another chance.

Although the arrival of the Mashiach and/or the resurrection of the dead will certainly surprise us, we will adjust. Neither event will change how we live. We will still have to eat, drink, find shelter and companionship, and learn in order to know. We will still have to strive in these endeavors, especially the learning. We will have to learn, grow, and actualize whatever we can before we die.

Looking back after death, we will realize—REAL-ize— that all these efforts were the basis for the blossoming of exquisite self-affirmation. After death, our awareness will increase, as testified by NDE's, and the best part of such awareness will be that it all came from our effort in this world. It was really worth it!

Epilog

My goal here has been to describe Hashem according to the reality we know. If I succeeded in describing reality, then I expected you and everyone else to agree to my approach. Everyone? Did everyone ever agree on anything? Well, lately, yes.

Inspired by Covid 19

I started writing this during the Covid 19 pandemic. For the first time in human history, practically the whole world chose a common behavior, a good behavior, of preserving life rather than economic power. The choices weren't made perfectly. I suspected from the outset that the lockdown cure might prove worse than the virus disease. But I respected the sentiments driving the decisions. I pray that Hashem rewards our good intentions with the wisdom to understand what we need to do better in the future. That will give us back the emotional prosperity we left behind.

The whole world behaved together! The whole world was willing to make sacrifices for a higher value. What a milestone achievement! It echoes a golden age. All major religions anticipate some golden age of human harmony. This first example of human harmony—shutting down to prevent virus spread—might be the stepping stone on which to build further. It is a sign Mashiach is coming.

In Western society, even secularists—people who were never religious, or at least think they never were (I told a little story in Chapter 8 that shows maybe they really are religious)—dream of achieving a golden age of humanity. They won't admit that this dream only arose from the Torah promise of Mashiach, yet they are so convinced they can achieve it that the idea seems to have permeated their soul—or their consciousness, as they prefer to call it. How did that hope blossom in the face of overwhelming evidence to the contrary such as humanity's relentless history of war and selfishness? Their conviction flies in the face of the evidence which makes it especially surprising since they insist they always follow the evidence.

My guess is: the evidence cannot suppress the capital R Reality that the Torah reveals for us. The Reality is that we have to live with hope. People just need to believe that things will get better, that we are building a better future for our children. Even when hope is not justified, secularists cling to it out of real necessity.

Original Inspirations

People envision this golden age in different ways—how it will come about and what it will feature once it arrives. Differences are to be expected from different religions and cultures. We Jews know the original vision, the one powerful enough to give rise to all the others. We have the duty to portray its Realistic nature at every opportunity. In order to do so, we must know it well.

The Jewish people have the respect of the entire world—sometimes begrudgingly, but it's there. Israel, by transforming a desert into an agricultural exporter and by pioneering so many technological innovations, has exemplified to the world that Hashem has provided enough for everyone to share. All we need to bring about a golden age is the global desire to achieve it.

How can we inspire such global desire? We need the will to see it done. Where there is a will, there is a way, goes the saying, but that kind of will has to be single-minded. Such single-mindedness can only emerge from a clear, very clear, awareness of the Reality at hand. My hope is that this work helps uncover the fullness of that Reality.

The Reality is—Hashem has a plan. Hashem has always had a plan and it is crucial to conduct yourself accordingly.

Every human has a part to play in this plan, whether they intend to or not, because Hashem, after all, is a clever enough designer to include everyone in the plan. But being included won't give you satisfaction if your inclusion was forced, not chosen. Your satisfaction will be highest when you chose which role to play.

To choose your role, you will need to understand the planner and the plan. It always works that way. I hope I have helped you get to work.

In A Nutshell

Hashem's nature is to create. The most creative thing Hashem could create is a subsidiary creator. That is us. We create many things, but more than anything, we create relationships. Each relationship builds our Self. Mitzvah instructions train us how to build positive Selves. Our ultimate reward will be an appreciation of the Self we have built. Hashem will enjoy that, too.

Above is my book in a nutshell. Following, are my Rambam-inspired 13 descriptions of reality.

1. Hashem created everything. The more there is, the greater a Creator is Hashem. That is why Hashem loves creating.

2. Before Creation, there was no raw material with which to create—only Hashem's imagination. Our reality is imagined by Hashem but that is as real as possible

3. Hashem has no body, meaning no limits. Endless details can be creatively imagined and still fit in. (PS. That means the limits we perceive for ourselves are sef-imagined, not necessarily true.)

4. Hashem's most creative idea is us in that we create with our mind, like Hashem does. We most often fulfill Hashem's plan by creating

relationships which, in turn, expand the Creation that Hashem is imagining. Hashem loves to do that—see point 1.

5. Relationships are complicated (like the rest of Hashem's Creation). We need guidance to form positive relationships and not destructive ones. Torah mitzvahs are that guidance.

6. People are born with different talents so that they can create in a unique way. Prophecy showcases the extreme range of talents granted. Prophets revealed best practises for fulfilling human creative potential.

7. In every range, someone is at the top and, for prophets, that was Moshe whose clarity about Hashem was the best humanly possible.

8. Moshe's five books and his oral explanation of them were the best possible transmission of his clarity.

9. The Jewish people, in every generation, have best preserved the transmission of Moshe's clarity.

10. When we ignore Torah instructions, Hashem steps in to manage reality so that we might still recover as positive an outcome as possible, given our choices to date.

11. Our real, final reward will be the deep satisfaction of all we have created. The magnanimity of that realization will require a new World To Come.

12. Before the World To Come, there will finally arise a leader, Mashiach, who will inspire everyone in this world to earn their fullest reward possible.

13. The dead will return to this world to earn the full rewards they were unable to earn in their original circumstances.

Appendix - Rambam's Preamble to the 13 Principles
(translation from Sefaria.com)
(printed for reader's convenience)

All Jews have a share in the World To Come: I have seen [fit] to speak here about many great and especially weighty fundamentals of faith.

You should know that masters of Torah have had differences of opinion regarding the good that comes to a person when he does the commandments that God commanded us through Moshe, our teacher—peace be upon him—and regarding the bad that will find him if he transgresses them—very many disagreements according to the difference in their intellects. And the reasonings about them have become greatly confused to the point that you will almost not find anywhere a man for whom this matter is clear. And you will not find a definitive thing about it with any person, excepting with much confusion:

The [first] group reasons that the good is the Garden of Eden and that it is the place where one eats and drinks without physical exertion and without effort; and that there [one finds] houses of precious stones and beds fitted with silk and rivers that flow with wine and fragrant oils and many things of this type. And [they reason] that the bad is *Gehinnom* and it is a place burning with fire, in which bodies are burned and people are afflicted with all types of afflictions, that are recounted at length. And this group has brought proof for their reasoning from the words of our rabbis, may their memory be blessed, and from verses of Scripture, the simple meaning of which—completely or partially—fits with what they are saying.

And the second group reasons and thinks that the anticipated good is the days of the Messiah—may it speedily be revealed—and that in that time, people will all be angels, all living and existing forever and they will become of larger stature and multiply and be powerful until they inhabit the whole world forever. And that Messiah—according to their thinking—will live [forever] with the help of God, may He be blessed. And [they reason] that in those days the earth will produce woven clothes and baked bread and many such things which are impossible. And [they also reason] that the bad is that a person not be in existence during those days and not merit to see it. And they bring proof from many statements that are found with the sages and from many verses in Scripture, the simple meaning of which is in agreement with what they are saying or with some of it.

And the third group will think that the good that is hoped for is the revival of the dead, and that is that a person will come to life after his death and will come back, together with his relatives and the members of his household, and eat and drink; and that he will not die again. And [they think] that the bad is that he will not come to life after his death, together with the ones that come back to life. And they bring a proof for this from many statements that are found in the words of the sages and from many verses in Scripture, the simple meaning of which indicates what they are saying or some of it.

And the fourth group will think that the intention of that which is to come to us for doing the commandments is physical rest and the attainment of worldly desires in this world, like the fat of the lands and many properties and many children and physical health and peace and security, and that the king will be from Israel and that we will rule over the ones that troubled us. And [they think] that the bad that gets to us if we deny the Torah is the opposite of these things, like that which we [experience] today during the time of the exile. And they bring a proof—according to their reasoning- from all of the verses in the Torah, from the curses and the other [sections], and from all of the stories that are written in Scripture.

And the fifth group—and they are many—join all of these matters together and say that that which is anticipated is that the Messiah will come and bring the dead back to life, and they will enter the Garden of Eden, and they will eat there and drink and be healthy all the days of the world.

But [about] this amazing issue—I mean, the World To Come—you will find few that in any fashion bring it to their mind to think [about it] or [ponder over] this fundamental or determine upon which matter this word applies—if it is the objective or one of the previous opinions is the objective, or to differentiate between the objective and the cause that leads to the objective. Rather what the entire people—the masses and the intelligentsia—ask about is how the dead will arise—naked or dressed; and whether they will arise with the same shrouds with which they were buried, with their embroidery and designs and beautiful stitchery, or with a cloak that only covers their bodies? [And they ask] when the Messiah will come, whether there will be rich and poor and if there will be the strong and the weak in his days, and many questions like these, all the time.

And you who look into this book, understand this parable that I am drawing for you and then prepare your heart and listen to my words about all of this. **Place it** in your mind that when they bring a young boy to a teacher to teach him Torah—and that is the greatest good for him as to what he can attain of wholeness—but due to his few years and the weakness of his intellect, he does not understand the level of this good and that which will come to him of wholeness from it. And therefore it is necessary for the teacher who is more whole to encourage his studies with things that are beloved to him due to the smallness of his years. And [so] he says to him, "Read and I will give you nuts or figs, and I will give you a little honey." And through this he will read and exert himself; not for the actual reading—as he does not know its value—but rather so that they will give him that food. And the eating of these delights is more precious in his eyes than the reading and great good—without a doubt. And so he thinks of the study as labor and effort, and he labors in it so that he will receive through this labor the objective that is beloved to him, and that is a nut or a portion of honey.

And when he grows and his intellect becomes stronger, and that thing that was (that will be) weighty for him before becomes light in his eyes and he goes to loving something else, they encourage him and arouse his desire for that thing that is beloved to him. And his teacher says to him, "Read and I will buy you fine shoes or lovely clothes." And through this, he makes efforts to read, not for the actual study, but rather for that garment; and that clothing is more weighty in his eyes than the Torah. And that is for him the objective of its reading.

And when he becomes more whole in his intellect and this thing becomes negligible in his eyes, [his teacher] will also place his mind on that which is greater than this. And then his master will tell him, "Learn this section or this chapter and I will give you a dinar or two dinars" And through this, he reads and exerts himself to get that money—and for him, that money is more weighty than the study, since the objective of the study for him is that he get the gold that they promised him for it.

And when his intellect is greater and this amount becomes light in his eyes and he knows that this is something insignificant, he will desire that which is weightier than this. And his master will tell him, "Study so that you will be a leader and judge, and people will honor you and rise in front of you—like with so and so and so and so." And he will read and exert himself in order to achieve this stature and the objective will be the honor; that people will honor him and raise him up and praise him.

And all of this is despicable. And, nonetheless, it is necessary because of the smallness of the human intellect that he makes the objective of wisdom something else besides wisdom, and say for what thing he is learning, and that is that honor will come to him. And this is [making] a laughingstock of the truth. And about such study the sages say it is not for its sake, meaning that he does the commandments and studies and exerts himself in Torah, not for that thing itself, but rather for the sake of something else.

And the sages warned us about this and said, (Avot 4:5), "Do not make it [the Torah] into a crown with which to aggrandize yourself, and not into a spade with which to dig into them." And they are hinting to that which I have explained to you; that there is no [ulterior] objective to wisdom—not to receive honor from people and not to earn money—and [so,] one should not be involved in the Torah of God, may He be blessed, to earn money, and there should not be an [ulterior] objective for him in the study of wisdom, except only to know it.

And so [too,] there is no objective to the truth except that he knows it is the truth, and that the Torah is the truth; and the objective of its knowledge is to do [what is in] it. And it is forbidden for a whole person to say, "When I do these commandments, which are good character traits; and I distance myself from sins, which are bad character traits—that God, may He be blessed, commanded not to do—what is the reward that I will receive for it?" As this is like that which the child will say, "When I read this, what will they give to me?" And they will say, "Such and such a thing." As when we see the smallness of his intellect that he doesn't understand the size [of what he is involved in], and we see that he asks for another objective, we answer him according to his foolishness; as it is stated (Proverbs 26:5), "Answer a fool according to his foolishness."

And the sages have already warned about this as well; that is to say that a person should not render any of the [various] things to be the objective of his service to God, may He be blessed, and the performance of the commandments. And this is what the whole man who grasped the truth of [these] things, Antigonos, the man of Sokho, said (Avot 1:3), "Do not be as servants who are serving the master in order to receive a reward, rather be as servants who are serving the master not in order to receive a reward." And indeed he wanted to say with this that one should believe in the truth for the sake of the truth; and this is the matter they call, 'one who serves from love.'

And they said, may their memory be blessed (Avodah Zarah 19a), "'His commandments desire greatly' (Psalms 112:1)—Rabbi Eliezer said, 'His commandments; and not the reward of His commandments.'" And how lucid is this and it is a clear proof for that which we have [written] above in the essay. And even greater than this is what they said in the Sifrei on Deuteronomy 11:13, "Lest you say, 'Behold, I am learning Torah so that I will be rich; so that I will be called, rabbi; so that I will receive reward in the World To Come; [for this reason] does the statement teach, 'to love the Lord, your God'—everything that you do, only do it out of love."

Behold, this matter has been clarified to you, and it has become clear that it is the intention of the Torah and the foundation of the intention of the sages, peace be upon them. And only a crazed fool will ignore this because silly thoughts and bad ideas have corrupted him and mixed him up. And this is the level of Avraham, our father—peace be upon him (Sotah 31a)—as he served from love. And towards this path, it is fitting that there be arousal.

And since the sages, may their memory be blessed, knew that this is a very difficult matter—and not every person can grasp it, and if he grasps it, he doesn't agree with it at the beginning of the matter, and reasons that it is not a clear belief—since a person will only do an act in order to achieve a goal or to prevent a loss, and if it is not so, that matter will be futile and empty for him; [if so] how can you say to one who follows the Torah, "Do these acts and don't do [other] ones," [but] not for the fear of punishment from God, may He be blessed, and not to inherit a goodly reward. This is a very difficult thing, since not all people grasp the truth, to the point that they [reach the understanding of] Avraham, our father—peace be upon him.

And therefore they permitted the masses—so that their faith will sit well—to do the commandments with the hope of reward, and to separate from the sins out of the fear of punishment. And we encourage them about this and strengthen their intentions [to do the commandments out of ulterior motives], until he grasps and knows what is the truth and the complete way; as we do with a child at the time that he studies, as we have brought in the parable. And they blamed Antigonos, the man of Sokho, for his explaining what he explained to the masses, and they said about this, "Be careful with your words," as is explained in Avot 1:11.

And the masses do not lose everything by doing the commandments out of fear of punishment and hope for reward, except that [their performance] will not be complete. And nonetheless, it is good for them, so that they have the ability and habit and effort of fulfilling the Torah. And from this, they will be aroused to know the truth, and they will turn into those that serve from love. And this is what they said, may their memory be blessed (Sanhedrin 105b), "Truly, a person should be involved in Torah and even not for its sake, as from 'not for its sake,' comes 'for its sake.'"

And it is from that which you must know that [with regards] to the words of the sages, may their memory be blessed, people are divided into three groups: **The first**—and it is most of what I have seen and of the compositions that I have seen and of what I have heard about—believes them according to their simple meaning, and does not reason that they have any sort of esoteric meaning. And for them, the impossible things must correspond to reality.

However, they do this as a result of their not understanding wisdom; and they are far from the sciences and they do not have wholeness so that they are aroused on their own and they did not find someone to arouse them. [These people] hold that the sages, may their memory be blessed, only intended in all of their straight and sweet words what [this group] understood according to their intellect from them, and that they are according to their simple meaning—and even though that which appears in some of their words is repulsive and that which pushes the intellect away. To the point that if it would be recounted to the unlettered—and all the more so to the wise—they would wonder in their pondering over them and say, "How is it possible that there is someone in the world that thinks like this or believes that it is a correct belief—all the more so, that it is good in their eyes?"

And one should be pained about the foolishness of this group of simple-minded ones. According to their opinion, they are honoring and raising the sages; but they are [in fact] lowering them to the lowest depths—and they do not understand this. And as God, may He be blessed, lives, this group destroys the beauty of the Torah and darkens its splendor, and makes the Torah of God the opposite of its intention. As God, may He be blessed, said in the perfect Torah (Deuteronomy 4:6), "that they should observe all of these statutes and they shall say, 'This is certainly a wise and understanding people, this great nation.'" And this group recounts the simple words of the sages, may their memory be blessed, such that when the other nations hear it, they say, "This is certainly a foolish and silly people, this small nation."

And the ones that do this the most are the preachers that explain and inform the masses of the people about that which they [themselves] do not know. And were it only that since they did not know and understand, they would be quiet, as it is said (Job 13:5), "Were it only that you would be silent, and it will be considered wisdom for you"; or that they would say, "We do not understand the intention of the sages in this statement and not how it is to be explained." But [instead], they think that they understand it and attempt to inform [about] it, to explain to the people what they understood according to their weak intellects—not that which the sages said—and they preach at the heads of the people the homilies from Tractate Berakhot and from the chapter [entitled] Chelek and from others, according to their simple meanings, word for word.

And the second group is also numerous, and they are the ones that saw the words of the sages or heard them, and understood them according to their simple meaning, and thought that the sages did not intend in them anything more than that which is indicated by the simple [understanding]. And they come to make them foolish and to disgrace them and to bring ill-repute to that which has no ill-repute, and they mock the words of the sages. And [they believe that] they are more refined in their intellect than [the sages], and that they, peace be upon them, were stupid, simple-minded fools regarding all of existence; to the point that they did not grasp matters of wisdom in any way.

And most of those that stumble in this error are those with pretense to the medical sciences and those that carry on about the laws of the constellations; since they are—according to their thinking—understanding and wise in their [own] eyes and sharp and philosophers. And how far are they from humanity, according to those that are truly wise and philosophers. Rather, they are more foolish than the first group, and many of them are idiots. And it is an accursed group since they question great and lofty people, whose wisdom was already made clear to the wise. And were these idiots to exert themselves in the sciences to the point that they would know how it is proper to organize and write things in the science of theology, and things which are similar to it, for the masses and for the wise, and they would understand applied philosophy; then they would understand if the sages, may their memory be blessed, were wise or not; and the matter of their words would be elucidated for them.

And the third is, as God lives, very small to the point that it is not fitting to call them a group except in the same way as one says about the sun that it is a species [even if] it is [in fact] unique. And these are the same people to whom the greatness of the sages, may they be blessed, and the quality of their intellect was made clear, from what was found among their words, [things] that indicate matters that are very true. And even though [these things] are few and scattered in different places in their compositions, they indicate their wholeness and that they grasped the truth; and that the impossibility of the impossible and the necessity of that which exists was also clear to them.

And [the members of the third group] knew that [the sages], peace be upon them, were not saying jokes; and it became established for them that [the sages'] words have a revealed and secret meaning and that in everything they said about things that are impossible, they were speaking by way of a riddle and a parable—since this is the way of great wise men. And therefore the greatest of wise men opened his book by saying (Proverbs 1:6), "To understand a parable and a metaphor, the words of wise men and their riddles." And it is known to the linguist that a riddle is when the matter intended by it is hidden and not revealed by it, and as it said (Judges 14,12), "I will tell you a riddle, etc." Since the words of the sages are all about supernal matters of ultimacy, they must then be riddles and parables.

And how can we blame them for writing wisdom in the way of parable and making it appear as lower things of the masses, when we see that the wisest of all men did this with the holy spirit—I mean Shlomo, in Proverbs and in the Song of Songs and in some of Ecclesiastes? And why should it be difficult for us to explain their words rationally and to take them out of their simple meaning in order that they fit reason and correspond to the truth. And even if they are holy writings, they themselves explain verses of Scripture rationally and take them out of their simple meaning and make them into parables.

And it is the truth, as we find that they said to explain the verse (I Chronicles 11:22), "he smote the two powerful lions of Moav," that it is all a parable; and so [too] that which is stated [further in the verse] "he descended and smote the lion in the pit" is a parable. And so [too] that which is stated (I Chronicles 11:17), "Who will give me water to drink from the well of Beit Lechem," and the entire story is all a parable (Bava Kamma 60b). And so [too] about the story of Iyov in its entirety, some of them said it was a parable (Bava Batra 15a), and they did not explain for what thing it was made a parable. And so [too], some of them said that the dead of Yechezkel was a parable (Sanhedrin 72b). And there are many [examples] like this.

And if you, the reader, are from one of the first two groups, do not pay attention to my words and not to any matter of it; since no part of it will be fit for you, but [rather] it will hurt you and you will hate it. For how can light foods that are few in quantity but proper in quality be fit for a person who is accustomed to bad foods—rather, in truth, they will hurt him and he will hate them. Did you not know what the people that were accustomed to eating onions and garlic and fish said (Numbers 21:5), "and our souls are disgusted, etc."? But if you are from the third group, [so that] when you see one of their words that intelligence pushes off, you stop and reflect about it and know that it is a riddle and a parable, and you lay burdened in your heart and occupied by the meaning of the idea in the composition and in its rational meaning and think to find the intelligent intention and the straight faith, as is stated (Ecclesiastes 12:10), "to find words of desire and written straightly, even words of truth"—and [if so], look into this book of mine and it will help you, with God's help.

And now I will begin to speak about that which I intended: You should know that just like the blind man does not grasp the appearance of colors and the deaf man does not grasp the sound of voices and the eunuch sexual desire, so too, bodies do not grasp spiritual pleasures. And just like the fish do not know the element of fire, since they are in the element of water, which is its opposite; so too, in this physical world, pleasures of the spiritual world are not known. Rather we do not have among us any of this pleasure, but only pleasures of the body and that which is grasped by the senses [regarding] food and drink and sex.

And anything besides these is non-existent for us and we do not recognize it. [Neither] do we grasp it at first thought, but only after great analysis. And it is fitting that it is like this, since we are in the physical world, and that is why we only grasp the lower temporary pleasures. But the spiritual pleasures are permanent, lasting forever, without end. And there is no connection or similarity in any way between these [two types] of pleasures.

And it is not fit for us, the masters of Torah, and not for the Godly of the philosophers that we should say that the angels or the stars or the spheres do not have any pleasure; but rather they truly have great pleasure in that they know and grasp the truth of the Creator, may He be blessed. And so [too], when the one that will be purified is purified and he goes up to that level after his death, he does not grasp the physical pleasures and does not want them. But rather it is similar to if a king who is at the top of the government would divest himself of his kingdom and his government and go back to playing ball with children like he used to do before his kingdom. Since that was in his being small of years when he did not distinguish between the worth of these two things; just as we today praise and elevate the physical pleasures and not the spiritual pleasures.

And when you reflect on the matter of these two pleasures, you will find the inferiority of the one and loftiness of the other—and even in this world. And that is because you will find that most people always tire themselves and their bodies in toil and exertion, that has no equal, in order that worth and honor come to him and that people elevate him. And this pleasure is not the pleasure of food and drink. And likewise, many people will choose to take revenge on their enemies rather than enjoy many physical pleasures. And [also] many people distance themselves from the greatest of the physical pleasures out of fear that disgrace and embarrassment from people come to him from this, or because he is seeking to have a good name.

And if its matter is such in this physical world, all the more so is it in the spiritual world; and that is the World To Come—that our souls will fathom there the knowledge of the Creator, may He be blessed, just like the supernal bodies fathom [Him] or more [so]. And this pleasure cannot be divided into sections and cannot be recounted, and you will not find a parable by which to compare this pleasure. But rather it is as the prophet, peace be upon him, said when the greatness of that good and its value were so wondrous in his eyes. He said (Psalms 31:20), "How great is Your goodness that You have hidden for those that fear You."

And so [too], they, may their memory be blessed, said (Berakhot 17a), "In the World To Come there is no eating and no drinking and no bathing and no anointing and no intercourse, but rather the righteous ones sit and their crowns are upon their heads and they derive pleasure from the radiance of the Divine Presence." He wants to say by stating, "and their crowns are upon their heads," the permanence of their soul in the existence of that which is fathomed by them, and that is the Creator, may He be blessed; and in that He—meaning that which is fathomed (the active Intellect)—and He are one thing, as the philosophers have mentioned in ways that are [too] lengthy for here.

And by their saying, "and they derive pleasure from the radiance of the Divine Presence," I would say that those souls derive pleasure in that which they grasp and know of the truth of the Creator, may He be blessed, like the holy creatures and the other levels of angels derive pleasure, in what they grasp and know of His existence. Behold, that the ultimate and good objective is to reach this supernal company and to be with this honor and the level mentioned, and the preservation of the soul—as we have explained—without an end, in the existence of the Creator, may He be blessed, Who is the cause of its existence, since [the soul] has grasped Him, as is explained by the first philosophers.

And this is the great good, to which there is no good to equate to it and no pleasure to compare to it, since how can the eternal that has no end and no finish be compared to something finite. And this is what it stated (Kiddushin 39b), "'In order that it will be good for you and you will lengthen your days' (Deuteronomy 22:7)—in the world that is completely long."

And the complete bad and great reprisal is that the soul be cut off and be destroyed and that it not be alive and existent. And this is the cutting off (karet) that is written in the Torah, as in (Numbers 15:31), "and that soul will surely be cut off (hikaret, yikaret)." And they, of blessed memory, said, "*Hikaret*—in this world, *yikaret*—in the World To Come" (Sanhedrin 64b). And it is stated (I Samuel 25:29), "the soul of my master shall be bundled in the bundle of life." Behold, in all that he chose and accustomed himself to the pleasures of the body and disdained truth and loved falsehood, his soul was cut off from this level and it remained cut off matter [after his death]. And the prophet, peace be upon him, already elucidated that the World To Come is not grasped by the physical senses and this is what is stated (Isaiah 64:3), "an eye has not seen, O Lord, except for You." And they said in explanation of this, "All of the prophets only prophesied about the days of the Messiah, but about the World To Come, 'an eye has not seen, O Lord, except for You'" (Berakhot 34b).

As for the matter of good outcomes and reprisals and bad (besides cutting off) that are written in the Torah, it is what I will explain to you. And it is that He says to you, "If you will do these commandments, I will help you with their performance and to be complete in them, and I will remove from you all of the obstacles and impediments." As it is impossible for a man to do the commandments for Him, when he is sick and hungry or thirsty and in a time of war and siege. And therefore He makes it come out that all of these matters will be removed, and that they be healthy and quiet until [their] knowledge is perfected and they merit life in the World To Come. Behold that the objective of the reward of doing [the precepts of] the Torah is not in all of these things. And so too, if they violate the Torah, the punishment of these bad things that will befall them is [so that] they will not be able to do the commandments; and as it is stated (Deuteronomy 28:47), "Since you did not serve."

And when you reflect upon this with complete reflection, you will find it is as if He says to you, "If you have done some of the commandments from love and with effort, I will help you to do them all, and I will remove from you the obstacles and impediments; and if you abandon one of them in the manner of disgracing [it], I will bring impediments to you that will impede you from them doing all of them, until you not have wholeness and existence in the World To Come. And this is the matter that they said, of blessed memory (Avot 4:2), "The payment (reward) of a commandment is a commandment and the payment of a sin is sin."

And the Garden of Eden, however, is a rich and fertile place—the choicest of lands. It has many rivers and fruit-bearing trees. God, may He be blessed, will reveal it to people in the future to come and show that way that leads to it, and they will enjoy it. And it is possible that they will find very wonderful plants that are very useful in it, besides the ones that are known and famous to us. And all of this is neither impossible nor unlikely, but rather it is likely—and even if had not been written in the

Torah; all the more so, since it is elucidated and publicized in the Torah.

Gehinnom, however, is the name for the pain and the punishment that will come to the evildoers, but the Talmud did not give a [definitive] description of this punishment. Rather, there are those that say that the sun will approach them and burn them, and their proof to this is from that which is stated (Malachi 3:19), "behold [the sun of] the day is coming, burning like a furnace." And there are some that say that a strange heating up will begin in their bodies and burn them, and their proof to this is from that which states (Isaiah 33:11), "your spirit is fire, it shall consume you."

And the revival of the dead is from the main fundamental principles of Moshe, our teacher—peace be upon him. And there is no religion and no attachment to the Jewish religion for the one who does not believe [in] this. But it is [only] for the righteous, and so [too] is [this found in] the language of Bereishit Rabbah, "The power of rain is for the righteous and for the evildoers, but the revival of the dead is only for the righteous." And how should the evildoers be revived—as they are dead even in their lifetime? And so [too] did they say (Berakhot 18b), "Evildoers are called dead even in their lives, righteous people are called living even in their death." And you should know that man, perforce, must die and decompose and return to what he is composed of.

The days of the Messiah, however, is the time when rulership will return to Israel and that they will go back to the land of Israel and that this king will be very great, and the seat of his rulership will be in Zion (Jerusalem). His fame will grow and his mention will be among all of the nations, [even] more than King Shlomo. And all of the peoples will make peace with him and all of the lands will serve him, due to his great righteousness and due to the wonders that will come about through him. And anyone that comes against him, God, may He be elevated, will deliver into his hand. And all of the [relevant] verses in Scripture testify to his success and our success with him. And nothing about existence will change from what it is now, except that rulership will return to Israel. And this is the language of the sages (Sanhedrin 91b), "There is no difference between this world and the days of the Messiah except for the subjugation by the nations alone."

And there will be in his days rich and poor, strong and weak, in relation to each other. But it will be very easy in those days for people to find their sustenance; to the point that with a little effort that a person exerts, a great output will result. And this is what they said (Shabbat 30b), "In the future, the land of Israel will produce loaves of bread and woolen garments"; since people say that when a person finds something prepared and ready, "So-and-so found baked bread and cooked food." And the proof to this is that which is stated (Isaiah 61:5), "and foreigners shall be your plowmen and your vintners," to show that there will [still] be planting and reaping. And therefore this sage who said this statement to his student got angry when [the latter] did not understand his words and thought that it was its simple meaning. And he responded to him according to his understanding and that answer was not a true answer. And the proof that he did not respond to him with a true answer is that he brought proof from (Proverbs 26:4-5), "Do not answer a fool according to his folly [... Answer a fool according to his folly]."

And the great objective that will occur in those days is that we shall rest from the subjugation by the nations which prevents us from the performance of all of the commandments; and that wisdom will grow, as it is stated (Isaiah 11:9), "since the earth will be full of the knowledge of the Lord." And the wars will cease, as it is stated (Micah 4:3), "and nation will not lift up sword against nation." And great wholeness will be found in those days and we will merit thereby life in the World To Come. But the Messiah will die and his son will reign in his place, and [likewise] his grandson. And the prophet has already elucidated his death: "He will not tire and will not be crushed until he puts justice in the world" (Isaiah 42:5). And his rulership will extend for very many days and the lives of people will also lengthen. Since when worries and troubles are removed, the days of a man are lengthened. And one should not wonder that his rulership will last for thousands of years, since the sages said about the gathering of good, that when it gathers, it will not quickly separate.

And we do not desire and hope for the days of the Messiah because of the multitude of produce and wealth and not [since] we will ride on horses and not [since] we will drink wine accompanied by types of song, as ones of confused intellect imagine. But [rather] the prophets and pious ones desired the days of the Messiah—and their longing for it grew—because of what will be in it from the gathering of the righteous and the proper administration and wisdom, and from the righteousness of the king and his great uprightness, and the heft of his wisdom and closeness to God, as it is stated (Psalms 2:7), "the Lord said to me, 'You are my son, I conceived you today'"; and the performance of all of the commandments of the Torah of Moshe, our teacher—peace be upon him—without negligence and laziness and without duress. As it is stated (Jeremiah 31:33), "And they will not continue to teach a man [to his brother and a man to his fellow] saying, 'Know the Lord,' since they will all know me, from their small ones to their big ones"; "and I have placed my Torah in their hearts" (Jeremiah 31:32); "and I will remove your heart of stone from your flesh" (Ezekiel 36:26). And there are many of these [types of] verses about this matter.

And through these matters, they would strongly attain [life in] the World To Come. And the objective is the

World To Come and towards it is the effort. And therefore this sage (the author of this Mishnah), who is established in his knowledge of the truth, investigated [what is] the ultimate objective and left that which was other than it, and said, "All Jews have a share in the World To Come." And [even] if it is the desired objective, it is not fitting for one who wants to be one who serves from love, that he should serve in order to reach the World To Come, as we have elucidated in what came before. But [rather], one should serve in the way that I will say. And that is that if he believes that there is wisdom, and it is the Torah which came to the prophets from the Creator, may He be elevated, who informed them through it of the virtues and they are the commandments and the defects and they are the sins, [then] it is fitting for him from the angle of his being a man of proper disposition that he should do the good and go away from the bad.

And when he does this, he achieves humanness and is distinguished from animals. And when a person is whole [like this], it is from the nature of the whole person that there not be an impediment for his soul to exist in the existence that is known for it, and that is the World To Come, as we have said. And this is [the meaning of] what is stated (Psalms 32:9), "Do not be like a horse, like a mule that does not understand, with a bit and a bridle is his mouth restrained" [to be] like the impediments of animals from impulses, which is something external, like a bit and a bridle. And it is not fitting for a person to be like this, but [rather] his impediment should be from him and from his essence. I mean to say that the human form when it is complete is what impedes him from those things that wholeness prevents, and these are called the defects. And [his form] will energize him and push him towards that which will bring him to wholeness and that is the virtues.

This is what has been clarified to me from all of their words about this lofty and weighty matter. And I will still write a composition in which I will gather all of the homilies that are found in the Talmud and in other [books] and I will elucidate them and analyze them such that they fit with the truth of [their] matters, and I will also give proofs [to this] from their words. And I will reveal which of the homilies are like their simple understanding and which are parables and which are dreams [even though] they are described in completely straightforward statements as if they were in a waking state. And in that composition, I will elucidate for you many beliefs and there I will elucidate all of the things of these principles that I have given to you a little [here, that you] extrapolate from them to the others. And one should not be exacting with me, that in this essay I have somewhat overlooked words and matters about which experts are exacting; since I have overlooked this exactitude to allow for understanding for the one that has no prior education in this lofty matter that not all people grasp.

And [concerning others enumerated by the Mishnah as not having a share in the World To Come,] the word, "*epikores*," is Aramaic. Its meaning is one who abandons (*mafkir*) and denigrates the sages or a specific Torah scholar or denigrates his teacher. And they said that "outside books" are the books of those who err and so [too] the book of Ben Sira—and he composed books that included buffoonery about matters of facial recognition. They do not have a reason or a point except for wasting time with vanities. For example, those books found by the Arabs of historical stories and the conduct of kings, the genealogy of the Arabs, songbooks, and the like are from the books that do not have any wisdom or physical benefit, except for wasting time.

"And one who whispers [an incantation] over a wound" [has no share in the World To Come]—and provided that it is with spit—because this involves a denigration of God, may He be blessed. And [likewise], one who pronounces the name [of God] with its letters, *yod, hay vav, hay*—which is the explicit name (*shem hameforash*). And they have already mentioned things besides these, that if one does them, he has no share in the World To Come: they said (Bava Metzia 59b), one who whitens the face of his fellow in public and one calls his fellow by his nickname and (Yerushalmi Chagigah 2:1) one who derives honor from his friend's disgrace. Since one would not do from these acts—and even though one might think them to be light sins—except for one with an inferior spirit that does not have wholeness and is not fitting for the World To Come.

And from that which is necessary that we mention here—and [here] is the most fitting of all places—is that the fundamental beliefs and the foundational principles of our religion are Thirteen Principles:

[after this Rambam elucidates his thirteen principles which I have re-named thirteen descriptions of reality]

Made in the USA
Middletown, DE
25 October 2022

13486060R00146